33

History
5/18

CIVIL WAR DOCTOR
THE STORY
OF
MARY WALKER

CIVIL WAR DOCTOR
THE STORY
OF
MARY WALKER

Carla Joinson

**MORGAN
REYNOLDS**
PUBLISHING
Greensboro, North Carolina

Social Critics and Reformers

Waging Peace: The Story of Jane Addams

Civil War Doctor: The Story of Mary Walker

Rebels and Revolutionaries: Voices of American Labor

Library of Congress Cataloging-in-Publication Data

Joinson, Carla.
  Civil War doctor : the story of Mary Edwards Walker / by Carla Joinson. -- 1st ed.
     p. cm. -- (Social critics and reformers)
  Includes bibliographical references and index.
  ISBN-13: 978-1-59935-028-8
  ISBN-10: 1-59935-028-9
  1. Walker, Mary Edwards, 1832-1919. 2. Women physicians--United States--Biography. 3. Physicians--United States--Biography. 4. United States--History--Civil War, 1861-1865--Medical care.   I. Title. II. Series.
  [DNLM: 1. Walker, Mary Edwards, 1832-1919. 2. Physicians, Women--United States--Biography. 3. American Civil War. 4. Women's Rights--history. 5. Military Medicine--history. 6. History, 19th Century. 7. History, 20th Century.   WZ 100 W183J 2006] R154.W18J65 2006
  610.92--dc22

                                              2006029053

Printed in the United States of America
First Edition

This book is dedicated to my mother, who always encouraged me to follow my dreams, rather than society's expectations. She has been, and remains, a pillar of support.

Contents

Dr. Mary Edwards Walker
(Courtesy of the Granger Collection)

one
INDEPENDENT SPIRIT

In 1862, a woman treating injured American Civil War soldiers captured the attention of a *New York Tribune* reporter. Impressed with her medical skills, the correspondent wrote,

> Her sex ought not to disqualify her for the performance of deeds of mercy to the suffering heroes of the republic. Dressed in male habiliments, with the exception of a girlish-looking straw hat, decked off with an ostrich feather . . . her reputation is unsullied, and she carries herself amid the camp with a jaunty air of dignity well calculated to receive the sincere respect of the soldiers . . . she can amputate a limb with the skill of an old surgeon, and administer medicine equally as well.

The woman featured in the report was Mary Edwards Walker, a volunteer Union surgeon who braved some of the most ferocious battle scenes of the American Civil War to provide medical care for the sick, injured, and dying. Walker's acts of gallantry earned her the Medal of Honor, the nation's highest honor, and set her on a life course that helped to break down barriers against women in the medical profession and beyond. Opinionated, stubborn, and unconventional (she wore men's pants, top hats, bow ties and top coats), Walker possessed a resilient and determined spirit that would sustain her when held captive as a prisoner of war and when publicly derided for her passionate crusades for dress reform and women's suffrage.

Mary Edwards Walker was one of six children—five girls and one boy — born to an open-minded farmer and carpenter named Alvah Walker and his wife, Vesta. Alvah Walker learned carpentry at age thirteen after dropping out of school to help support his widowed mother and seven younger brothers and sisters. At age nineteen, he left his home in Greenwich, Massachusetts, and headed west. He returned home four years later, having witnessed slavery on cotton plantations in the South, listened to the bellows of alligators in Louisiana, and sailed on the brig *Oliver* through the Gulf of Mexico.

At age twenty-three, Alvah Walker married twenty-year-old Vesta Whitcomb. The couple moved to Syracuse, New York, then a new settlement on the Erie Canal, and he built the first frame house in their village.

This engraving shows the central part of Syracuse, New York, as it looked in 1841.
(Courtesy of the Granger Collection)

The young couple settled into family life, attending church services and visiting with family. Alvah Walker carved clock cases and small chests to earn money. After contracting measles as a child and suffering several bouts of its lingering complications as an adult, he also began reading medical books, and he gave up liquor and tobacco.

The Walker's first child, a son, lived only a few days. They buried the infant in a coffin built by Alvah. A year later, a daughter, Vesta, was born, and then came Aurora, Luna, and Cynthia.

After ten years in Syracuse, the family moved to a thirty-three-acre farm in Oswego Town, a community located about five miles west of Oswego, New York. Oswego lay on the edge of Lake Ontario and was a bustling center for commerce. It was a boomtown that teemed with progressive ideas, reform movements, and freethinking people. In 1832, the population there was 3,000 and by the start of the Civil War in 1861, the population was more than 17,000. Much of this growth could be attributed to Oswego's key position between bodies of water, both natural and manmade, such as a canal linking the Erie Canal with Lake Ontario at Oswego Harbor.

Alvah Walker cleared his farmland and built a house, barn, and the first schoolhouse in Oswego.

This photograph of the Walker homestead was taken in 1920. The house burned down in 1923. (Courtesy of Oswego County Historical Society)

Three months after the family moved to the farm, on November 26, 1832, Mary Edwards Walker was born. She was named Edwards after her mother's sister in Massachusetts. A year later, the couple welcomed a son.

Alvah Walker was forward-thinking for his time, in that he allowed his girls to study and pursue professional careers. In the mid-nineteenth century, women could not vote, own property, and many men believed women were intellectually inferior and denied them higher education. The job of raising children belonged exclusively to women, who, in turn, taught their daughters to cook, clean, and care for children, in preparation for when a girl married and continued the cycle. Considered the weaker sex, women were not expected to aspire to more than marriage and motherhood.

Alvah Walker disagreed. He also had unorthodox notions about how his daughters should dress. Most women wore long skirts made of yards of heavy fabric, tight corsets that created an hourglass figure, and high-heeled shoes. However, the Walker girls shared chores on the family farm, and none were required to wear corsets, which would have restricted their freedom of movement.

Farmwomen seldom followed fashion trends except in the few outfits they could wear to church or social engagements. They generally wore cotton or wool dresses with another light dress called a shift or chemise, underneath. Physically demanding chores such as chopping wood, cooking over wood stoves, tending a kitchen garden and churning butter required sturdy bodies and no-nonsense clothing.

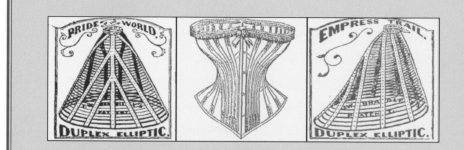

Dress Reform

While in medical school, Mary Edwards Walker had begun wearing a knee-length skirt over loose pants extending to the ankle. This fashion, sometimes called "pantaloons," had originated in a socialist commune of the 1820s called New Harmony. But it was made famous by Elizabeth Smith Miller, the daughter of Gerrit Smith, a leading businessman and property-owner in Oswego, and Amelia Jenks Bloomer. Bloomer advocated this style in her biweekly newspaper, *The Lily*, published from 1848 to 1854. Because of its exposure in Bloomer's publication, the outfit came to be known as "bloomers," and it sparked what became known as the "Bloomerite" movement.

The issue of what women wore was not a trivial matter in Walker's time. As late as 1917, when the U.S. entered World War One, women's clothing was burdensome and restrictive. Tight corsets were the fashion, as were long dresses with at least three petticoats underneath. A petticoat was an underskirt, starting at the waist, which was usually decorated with ruffles or lace. The more petticoats, the more shapely a woman appeared, the puffed-out dome of her skirt accentuating her waistline and bustline. This was the fashion even though multiple petticoats were heavy and could be unbearably hot in warm weather.

Dresses gradually became so full in the skirt that women could barely board trains or carriages without knocking someone else out of the way. Long dresses were clumsy, and corsets restricted a woman's flow of blood and often caused faintness. They also squeezed and displaced her internal organs, which led to heart palpitations, rapid breathing, and digestive problems. Sometimes corsets were so taut that they broke the rib cage. Even children and babies wore corsets, though this practice was dying out by the 1830s.

Dress reform for women was only one of the new movements beginning to stir in the United States in the mid-nineteenth century, particularly in New England and in upstate New York. The first Women's Rights Convention was at Seneca Falls, New York, in 1848, when Mary was sixteen. Also in 1848, a "free-love" colony was set up in Oneida, New York. Other movements were part of the intellectual life of the times: spiritualism, or attempts to communicate with the dead in a spirit world; abolitionism, or the drive to outlaw slavery in the United States; and temperance, or discouraging the drinking of alcohol and even attempting to make it illegal. There were also experiments in communal living, where all in the commune shared food, resources, and work. Reformers like Walker foresaw a future in which women would be freer in several ways, women's dress being a central issue.

However, in 1856, a startling contraption called the cage crinoline came into fashion. Made of steel, these cages rounded out from the waist to support dresses independently, so women did not need to wear so many heavy petticoats in order to achieve the massive volume then in fashion.

Instead, the cage held up the yards of cloth needed for their skirts, allowing women to walk freely underneath it. But the cage crinolines had drawbacks. They still required one petticoat so the steel ribs of the cage would not show, and because wind could get up under the cloth-covered cage, women had to wear long under garments to hide their legs. A sudden or clumsy move could cause damage and break things if they swung and hit an object with the steel cage. But this was the best new fashion advancement to come along in years, and the crinoline became very popular in the U.S., Britain, and France.

Despite their improvement, crinoline cages (also called hooped skirts) did not provide the freedom and comfort many women wanted. Walker never wore one and often pointed out their awkwardness: "If hoops are worn, there is atmospheric pressure to overcome . . . in the front, when walking against the wind, and the same to *resist* when walking from it." She continued to wear versions of the bloomer type of dress she had concocted in medical school, believing it the healthiest style she could choose. Walker also argued that excessive clothing caused illness and deformity in women, and contributed to marriage problems because women never felt completely well.

Dress-reformer Dr. Lydia Sayer had been a Bloomerite since 1849 and had begun practicing medicine in Washington the year before Walker finished medical school. She had also launched a publication called *The Sibyl: A Review of the Tastes, Errors and Fashions of Society.* In ancient Greek and Roman mythology, the sibyls were women prophets.

Sayer's publication gave women like Walker an opportunity to share their ideas with a sympathetic audience. Walker began writing to it in 1857 to promote her ideas about women's dress. These letters and her introduction to the Reform-Dress Association may have been her first taste of publicity.

Some of Walker's written material in *The Sybil* made it into the program of the second Reform-Dress Association's convention, and she affiliated herself with the organization for several years. In 1860, she was one of nine vice-presidents elected at the National Dress Reform Association Convention. The June 15, 1860, issue of *The Sybil* reported on the annual convention, and one of its resolutions included the following: "Resolved, That we can never expect women to be recognized the equal of man, until she emancipates herself from a dress which is both the cause and sign of her vassalage."

In a diary entry dated April 1870, Alvah Walker details the more than thirty tasks he did himself, including chopping wood, skinning animals, and performing repairs. He was seventy-two years old when he made the entry.

Alvah's liberal views about the role of women in society and his work as an abolitionist ignited a spirit of independence in his daughter Mary, who throughout her long life challenged accepted ways of thinking about women, and what they could and could not do.

In 1850, after attending the elementary school built by her father, eighteen-year-old Mary Walker attended Falley Seminary, an academy in the nearby town of Fulton. There she studied algebra, arithmetic, natural philosophy, grammar, physiology and hygiene, and Latin. She remained there for two terms.

Mary Walker (right) *and her sister Vesta, circa 1845.* (Courtesy of Oswego County Historical Society)

After leaving Falley Seminary, Walker taught school in Minetto, New York, a village five miles from Oswego. However, in 1853, she decided to give up teaching and return to school to become a doctor. She was twenty-one.

The profession of medicine was still in its formative years. Educational requirements for medical doctors varied among institutions. Doctors did not have to have a license to practice or even go through a prescribed education. Interested men could act as an apprentice for a few years and then open their own practice. However, with the formation of the American Medical Association in 1847, six years before Walker entered medical school, women were being excluded more and more even though they had been involved in health care since colonial times, including being midwives and delivering babies. Thus, two conflicting trends—to clamp down on the profession and to open it up to new practices—were at work when Walker decided to go into medicine.

In addition to inconsistency in training, there was disagreement about what constituted good practice. "Heroic" medicine, the traditional kind, included the antiquated practice of bloodletting (cutting the patient and draining "bad" blood off), inducing vomiting, blistering the skin, and prescribing substances now known to be toxic, such as mercury. Doctors trained in these practices were known as "regular" doctors.

The "non-regular" doctors were introducing milder treatments. These might include a healthier diet, herbal remedies, and homeopathy, which is treating a disease by using very small amounts of a remedy that in larger amounts would produce in a healthy person the same symptoms being treated in the sick person. Using a combination of techniques was called "eclecticism."

Institutions teaching "non-regular" medicine also favored including women. In 1849, Elizabeth Blackwell became the first woman in the United States to earn a medical degree from Geneva Medical College in Geneva, New York, and in 1853 Syracuse Medical School admitted Walker.

When Walker entered Syracuse Medical School, it had not been open long. The course of instruction consisted of three terms, thirteen weeks each. Tuition was fifty-five dollars a term. Walker studied as many as twelve different subjects related to medicine, such as anatomy and physiology, surgery, obstetrics, diseases of women and children, and pharmacy. Between terms, students were to work with a practicing physician. Walker attended the winter and spring terms from 1853 to 1855 and was awarded her degree in June 1855—the only woman in her graduating class.

While at Syracuse Medical School, Walker had also fallen in love with Albert Miller, a fellow student. He was older than most of the other students and was considered dashing, sociable, and a gifted public speaker. He was one of the speakers at their commencement. After graduation, however, Miller and Walker went their separate ways, he to practice medicine in Rome, New York, and she to practice in Columbus, Ohio, where her father's sister, Harriet Walker Hall, lived.

However, only a few months after graduation, in 1856,

Dr. Mary Walker's diploma from Syracuse Medical College. (Courtesy of Oswego County Historical Society)

Walker returned to Oswego and married Miller. The ceremony took place at the family home, and instead of asking the local Methodist minister to officiate, Walker chose a well-known Unitarian theologian. The Unitarians are a Protestant denomination known for their unorthodox views such as not believing in the divinity of Jesus. They supported reform issues of the day, including the abolition of slavery.

Besides an unconventional minister, Walker chose an

unconventional bridal outfit—trousers and dress-coat. She did not give the usual bride's promise to "obey" her husband, and she retained her maiden name. In the future, she would sometimes include "Miller" or "M" before "Walker," and would sometimes sign her name "Miller-Walker" or "Dr. Mary E.M. Walker."

Despite these irregularities in their marriage ceremony, Walker made clear in both her writings and speeches that she considered marriage a valuable and sacred institution. She paired with Miller in a joint medical practice in Rome, New York. However, their marital and medical union would prove short-lived.

two

REJECTING CONVENTIONS

Walker was a traditionalist in many ways. She supported marriage, duty to her country, and religion. L. Worden, a boarder with Walker and Miller, described Walker as self-reliant and noble, as well as a caring wife.

Walker's marriage, however, came to an end when she learned that Miller had been unfaithful, cheating on her with another woman. When she told him that she wanted a divorce, Miller suggested that she might prefer to "have the same privileges" he had exercised rather than leave him. This offer only served to make Walker angrier. Rather than accept her husband's infidelity or suffer in silence, Walker chose to leave him and seek a divorce.

Walker took a very serious step in refusing to live with her husband, and an even more serious one in contemplating divorce. A divorced woman usually lost her social status and could become an outcast. Without a husband's income and protection, she was also at the mercy of a society that did not believe women should work or live alone.

But Miller had been unfaithful to her, and that was a betrayal Walker did not take lightly. "He told me that if I would not get a bill of divorce, I could have the same privilege of infidelity," said Walker. "I could never live with a man who could make such a vile proposition to his wife."

This marital breech altered Walker's outlook on men and marriage. Although still young, she chose to cut herself off from romantic relationships. "Nothing can make an individual more wretched than to lose confidence," she said. "It is not simply that which is lost in the one person, but the distrust that is felt in all humanity." Walker considered marriage a necessary part of society, but she understood that men generally had the upper hand under the law. Divorces were difficult to obtain, and she spent ten years trying to get one.

In 1870, she wrote *Hit*, a book combining a number of essays on marriage, divorce, dress reform, and other subjects. "To be deprived of a Divorce is like being shut up in a prison because someone attempted to kill you," she wrote. "The wicked one takes his ease and continues his course, and you take the slanders, without the power to defend yourself."

Walker remained in Rome, New York, but moved into smaller rooms where she could live and work. Though many people scoffed at the idea of a female physician, a city paper, the *Rome Sentinel*, wrote, "Those . . . who prefer the skill of a female physician . . . have now an excellent opportunity to make their choice."

Walker was successful enough to keep herself housed and fed, but she had interests other than business. This middle part of the century was a turbulent time, and she thrived on new ideas. Women's rights, dress reform, and female education were hot-button issues for some people. Other changes were brewing as well. The idea that slavery was an evil and should be eradicated gained strength.

In 1859, militant abolitionist John Brown made a daring raid upon the federal arsenal at Harper's Ferry, Virginia. He had planned the attack for a long time and even asked former slave and abolitionist Frederick Douglass to help him. "I told him, and these were my words," said Douglass, "that he was going into a perfect steel trap and once in he would never get out alive."

Brown attacked the arsenal anyway, hoping to seize its 10,000 guns and use them to arm slaves. Brown's army consisted of twenty-two men, including five black men. They managed to capture the arsenal but were quickly overpowered. Ten were eventually killed, and five escaped. Brown and the six captives were tried and hanged.

Although it was a miserable failure, Brown's raid frightened the South and supporters of slavery in the North. Headlines in the October 18, 1859, issue of the New York *Herald* screamed "Fearful and Exciting Intelligence"; "Negro Insurrection at Harper's Ferry"; and "Arms Taken

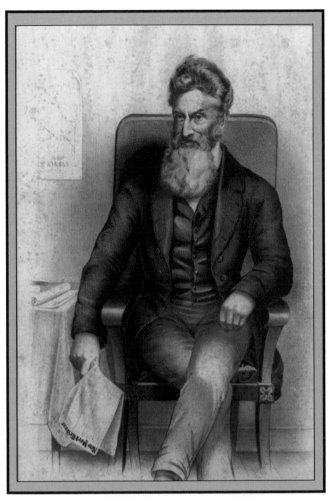

John Brown, leader of the failed attack on Harper's Ferry. (Library of Congress)

and Sent into the Interior," among other alarming pronouncements. Brown's raid crystallized the public's attention on how hot the passion over slavery had become and how society was changing over the issue.

Abraham Lincoln won the presidency in 1860. At the time, the economy of the industrial North boomed, fueled by cheap immigrant labor. Southern politicians, however, saw the election of Lincoln as trouble and a threat to their way of life. One southern state after another began to secede from the Union. The first state to secede was South

Carolina, on December 20, 1860, followed by Mississippi, Florida, Alabama, Georgia, Louisiana, and Texas. In all, eleven southern states would declare their secession from the Union and form the Confederate States of America.

Most southerners did not own slaves; still, they supported the view that each state should have the right to decide its own policies, rather than adhere to dictates from the federal government in Washington, DC. Numbers of Confederates took up arms for the principle of states' rights and to prevent Northerners, or Yankees, from invading their home states. Northerners fought to preserve the Union and to end slavery, which many considered morally evil.

State loyalties during the American Civil War.

Historians still debate the causes of the war, but central to any discussion of the conflict are the complex issues of states rights versus federal power, the institution of slavery, the expansion of slavery into new territories, and the preservation of the Union.

Regardless of the causes, tensions came to a boil in April 1861, when Confederate General P. G. T. Beauregard, who commanded provisional troops in South Carolina, demanded the surrender of Fort Sumter, a Union garrison, in Charleston Harbor. When Sumter's commander, Major Robert Anderson, refused to surrender, General Beauregard ordered artillery batteries to begin firing on Fort Sumter on April 12th.

The American Civil War had begun, and Mary Walker responded with patriotic determination. Her experiences during the war would change her life and reveal to a nation that a woman could offer many benefits to society outside the home.

three

"I Cannot Appoint a Woman"

No one was ready for a war. The North, with its superior weapons and larger population, was certain it would only take one decisive battle to convince the Confederates that their cause was doomed. The young fighting men of the Confederacy were convinced their bravery and fighting spirit would quickly vanquish a Union army made up of short-term volunteers and draftees. Expecting a short war, few bothered to put the infrastructure in place that would move supplies efficiently, take men where they needed to go, and look to their needs after a battle. Neither side expected the magnitude of the war that was about to begin.

The first intimation of what the future held came on July 21, 1861, when Confederate and Union troops engaged in a sharp confrontation that scattered wounded men across the battleground near Bull Run Creek in Virginia. In Washington, D.C., civilians were excited about the big battle and wanted to see the action before the war was over. Some hired carriages and made up picnic baskets so they could travel to the battlefront and watch the fighting. The battle was much more vicious and bloody than anyone expected, and when the Union troops were defeated, the terrified civilians fled back to Washington, followed by many panicked troops.

An artistic interpretation of the clash between Union General McDowell and Confederate General Beauregard at the Battle of Bull Run. (Library of Congress)

In the 1860s, Washington, D.C., had not yet become metropolitan. Despite the impressive building to the far right of the image, this sidewalk and dirt street are strewn with trash. (Library of Congress)

The inadequacy of Union preparation was suddenly apparent. No one had planned for evacuation. Soldiers with light wounds walked twenty miles to Washington, D.C. Ambulances belonged to the Quartermaster Corps, which handled supplies, and because their drivers refused to take orders from doctors, many severely wounded patients did not get picked up. The wounded, separated from their units, poured into Washington to hunt or beg for food and water.

When the war began, Washington, D.C. was only a dismal little city caught geographically between the North and South. There were only a few decent public buildings, and city residents dumped their chamber pots and garbage into the street and threw dead animals into the city canal. Vendors peddled fish and oysters on the street corners, and hogs roamed freely and plopped into muddy wallows on Capitol Hill and Judiciary Square. Following the chaos of the battle, the streets were filled with misplaced, needy people.

Mary Walker, by this time almost thirty years old, offered her services. Hoping to serve as an assistant surgeon, she journeyed in October 1861 to Washington, D.C., looking for a vacancy in one of its various hospitals. The Patent Office, a large government building, served as a makeshift hospital. There she met Dr. J. N. Green. "He stated that his predecessor had died from over work," said Walker. "He . . . had himself applied to Surgeon General Finley for an assistant in the hospital, but had been answered that there were none that he could give him."

Although surgeons were desperately needed, General Finley turned down Walker's application to serve as an assistant surgeon, saying, "I cannot appoint a woman."

Walker was disappointed but not deterred. She returned to the Patent Office and told Dr. Green, "I will work as your assistant without an appointment."

Green was grateful for the help. Walker made rounds in the hospital and prescribed medicine. She walked up and down long flights of stairs to meet the ambulances, examined and recommended treatment for patients, distributed medicine, and roused herself from bed at all hours to care for patients—all without pay.

The U.S. Patent Office in Washington, D.C., housed a hospital during the war.
(Library of Congress)

The slaughter and suffering of the Civil War demanded changes in traditional nursing care. In the past, male enlisted men recovering from an illness or injury nursed the few patients in military hospitals. Now, as wounded men poured into overflowing civilian hospitals, the old method no longer worked.

Women rose to meet the new challenge of providing care in military hospitals. Their efforts might have shocked the military establishment, but it was a logical development. At home, women almost always cared for their sick or injured relatives. Doctors were, however, the medical authorities outside the home, and battlefields were clearly their sphere of influence. Male surgeons made it plain that they did not want women invading their territory. However, the crisis was so overwhelming that their opposition did not matter. Women flooded into areas where battles had been fought, anxious to find and care for their loved ones. They crowded into makeshift hospitals with food and bandages, wrote letters for men too weak to hold pens, fed them, washed their faces, and read them newspapers

Some military physicians demanded that women leave their hospitals even though there was a shortage of male nurses. Equally determined women demanded the right to care for the wounded. "No one knows, who did not watch the thing from the beginning, how much opposition, how much ill will, how much unfeeling want of thought, these women nurses endured," wrote Georgeanna Woolsey, a battlefield nurse. "Hardly a surgeon of whom I can think,

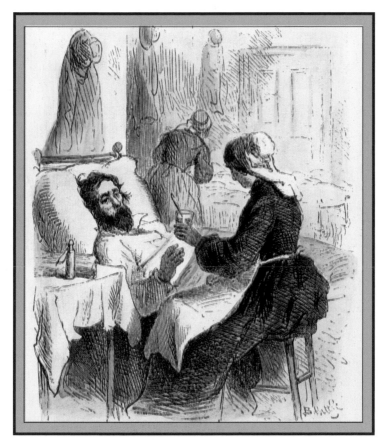

This engraving, published during the Civil War, suggests that the public had embraced the idea of women working as nurses in Union hospitals. (Library of Congress)

received or treated them, with even common courtesy . . . and the army surgeons . . . determined to make their lives so unbearable that they should be forced in self-defense to leave."

Short of throwing these women in jail or using force to keep them away, there was little military doctors could do. At first, these amateur nurses were family members or women in the community. Catholic nuns, almost universally accepted as nurses even by army doctors, also performed nursing services. Eventually the War Department allowed a civilian organization of nurses, the Women's Nursing Bureau, to provide nursing care for soldiers. Nurses were paid forty cents a day.

In 1861, the secretary of war appointed Dorothea Dix as superintendent of nurses. Dix's background as an advocate for prison reform and for better treatment of the mentally ill had prepared her well for the position.

As head of the Women's Nursing Bureau, Dix had definite ideas about what she wanted from nurses. They needed to be older than thirty-five, plain looking, obedient, and willing to wear dresses of brown, black, or gray, without any ornamentation. Dix proposed these restrictions in order to make the nurses more acceptable to the doctors. Dix had met Florence Nightingale, a famous British nurse who had revolutionized patient care during the Crimean War the decade before by cleaning up hospitals and demanding professional nursing care for wounded soldiers. Her advocacy had saved thousands of lives, and Dix admired her work.

Many hospitalized men described their female nurses as angels for their sympathetic attitudes and helpfulness. Doctors, however, were usually not popular. In the training camps as well as on the battlefields, doctors carried out a crusade against soldiers who pretended to be sick to avoid duty.

Field medicine was hurried and improvised, and care in regular hospitals was not much better. Doctors performed surgeries without any gloves or disinfectant, and tools were reused from patient to patient with virtually no washing.

Conscientious doctors did the best they could with the medicines in their possession, although many concoctions proved ineffective. A favorite army medicine, a mercury compound called calomel, was used to induce bowel movements. Using it too often could make soldiers lose their teeth. On the other hand, opium, an addictive narcotic, was good for bowels that were too loose. Doctors used both medicines freely.

Army medical provisions were also often in short supply and delivered late. Even more troubling was the fact that few cures existed for even the most common illnesses.

Neither military nor civilian doctors knew much about bacteria or disinfectants. In the case of military doctors, this lack of knowledge meant that they often spread infection while going from patient to patient in bloodied gowns and with unclean hands. Although civilian doctors had the same imperfect standards, they did not see as many wounded as military doctors.

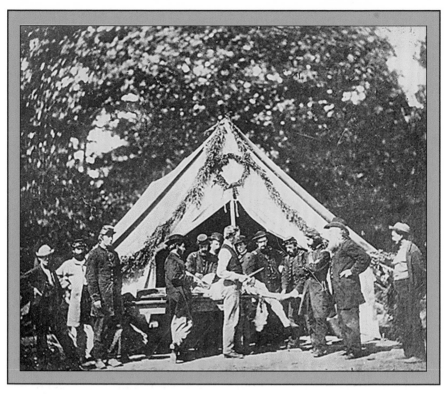

This open-air leg amputation took place after the battle of Gettysburg. (National Archives)

Surgeries were performed in rooms, in tents, or under the open sky and ran like a production line. Patients were fetched from the waiting crowd, jostled onto a table, given ether, which did not always put them completely out, and immediately sliced open. When the limb had been cut to the bone and the tissue scraped away, the doctor sawed the bone until the amputated limb fell off. It was tossed into a pile and the doctor would yell, "Next!"

Men writing in their diaries described these scenes as butchery and accused doctors of being uncaring or incompetent. Soldiers wrote about gruesome battlefield wounds being infested with maggots, and other horrors.

"I had assisted in an operation where there was amputation of an arm where it was no more necessary than to amputate anybody's arm that had never been injured," Walker wrote. "The two surgeons in the ward who had decided to have that arm amputated when there had been only a slight flesh wound, seemed to me to take this opportunity to amputate for the purpose of their own practice, which was utterly cruel."

Walker knew that she could not openly oppose any of the doctors or she would lose her place entirely. "I then made up my mind that it was the last case that would occur if it was in my power to prevent such cruel loss of limbs," she said.

Instead, she began to seek out patients scheduled to have limbs amputated. She would examine the injured and almost always determine that the procedure was unnecessary. She then coached the patients, privately, on how to protest against amputation. If a doctor insisted, she advised the men to "swear and declare that if they forced him to have an operation that he would never rest after his recovery until he had shot them dead."

Her strategy worked, and she took pride in knowing that she saved the arms and legs of soldiers. Her effort also saved the government money, by eliminating the need for disability pensions for amputees.

Despite the stress and intensity of her work, Walker enjoyed her time at the Patent Office hospital. In a letter to her brother and sisters, she said she visited Virginia and found the bridge at Arlington Heights impressive, as well as the many camp tents set up along the Potomac River. She admired the marble Patent Office building with its gaslights and mentioned seeing some of George Washington's personal property on display there. "I am assistant Physician and Surgeon in this Hospital," she wrote. ". . . Every soul in the Hospital has to abide by my orders as though Dr. Green gave them, and not a soldier can go out of this building after stated hours, without a pass from him or myself."

Had she been a full surgeon, Walker would have had the title of "major" and would have made one hundred sixty-nine dollars a month. As an assistant surgeon, the rank would be "captain" or "first lieutenant" at a salary of one hundred to one hundred thirty dollars a month. A contract surgeon with no officer's rank would make eighty to one hundred dollars, and an acting assistant surgeon would be paid similarly but would be considered a civilian. A nurse would make twelve dollars, but Walker did not want to be hired as a nurse.

She saw, treated, and prescribed medicine for at least a hundred patients a day, relieving Dr. Green of some of his overwhelming hospital tasks. In her spare time, she visited patients to cheer and comfort them. She supplied them with paper and ink, so they could write to their families, and for those too weak or injured, she wrote their dictated letters. The men appreciated her efforts and spoke highly of her. Walker also became skilled at requesting supplies, and she did not shy away from asking for anything, including hundreds of checkerboards, for her recuperating patients. Although she had not yet won the appointment to be an assistant surgeon, Walker persevered. Men who refused to recognize her abilities eventually found that her services were indispensable.

As 1861 drew to a close, Walker still had no official appointment, so she decided to go to Forest Hall Prison in Georgetown, where 6,000 Confederate prisoners of war were held. From there, she moved to a Union Deserters Prison in Alexandria. She had moved from one place to another, believing that the needs at each would prove so great she would finally be granted a commission as a physician. She was wrong, however, and cut short her stay at both places.

four

WORKING
WITHOUT PAY

Walker knew she could not work indefinitely without a paycheck. Dr. Green had offered to share his salary with her, but she declined because he had a wife and children. Because she was serving unofficially, she was free to come and go as she pleased. In January 1862, she left Washington and returned to New York. There she studied for one term at another unconventional medical school, Hygeia Therapeutic College in New York City. The program at Hygeia stressed natural cures instead of the "heroic" treatments still popular among more conventional physicians. She also liked that the school stressed the practice of good hygiene, a revolutionary medical idea in the mid-nineteenth century.

Even though Florence Nightingale had lowered the death rate in Crimean War hospitals from forty percent to two percent by stressing cleanliness, the practice still did not catch on in U.S. hospitals during the Civil War. Her work appealed to many women, and Walker's experiences probably helped her appreciate Nightingale's, and Hygeia's, approach to patient care.

When Walker completed her studies at Hygeia, she returned to Oswego in October 1862. There she wrote articles on dress reform, lectured, and tried to figure out how to obtain a commission to return to the war. Restless, she finally decided to go back to Washington. Physicians and patients welcomed her return to Washington, but the men who could have granted her a paid commission continued to ignore Walker's requests.

For her return to service, Walker designed a military-style outfit. She wore gold-striped pants similar to those of

Dorothea Dix (left) *and Florence Nightingale* (right) *helped reform medical tradition to allow women to nurse wounded soldiers.* (Library of Congress)

Dr. Mary Walker as she looked in her military-inspired dress during the war.
(Courtesy of Oswego County Historical Society)

an officer, and a surgeon's green sash. She also designed a hat with gold cord and an officer's overcoat.

In November 1862, she headed to Warrenton, Virginia, where many of the men who fought at the Battle of Antietam lay sick and wounded. Although Walker had seen the horrors of war while volunteering at the Patent Office hospital, now she would be even closer to the realities of war. She would serve in field hospitals, where the wounded received medical attention on the battlefield. The wounded would then go on to the field hospital, set up in tents, farmhouses, barns, and other makeshift structures. Some wounded would be sent by ambulance to hospitals in nearby towns or in Washington, while field surgeons would treat others.

Field surgeons had to hurry with their work. If they could amputate within twenty-four hours of an injury, only one man in four died. If they amputated after more than twenty-four hours, two in four died. As thousands of men poured in with shattered arms and legs, the amputation tent became an assembly line without time for gentleness or sympathy.

Though doctors often amputated unnecessarily, in the opinion of some including Walker, the nature of the men's wounds and the state of medicine at the time often required drastic measures. An innovation in warfare called the "minie ball" flattened when it hit flesh, instead of passing through the way other bullets did. The ball banged and splintered its way through bone, muscle, and flesh, leaving extensive damage that could not be repaired. The shattered limb had to be

In this small group of Union wounded, the man to the left of the image has had his right arm amputated and the soldier lying in the foreground has lost a leg below the knee. (National Archives)

amputated to save the patient's life. If, instead, he were transferred to a hospital, the risk of infection would be great.

Walker wanted to work at the field hospitals. Hoping to win an appointment as a surgeon by proving her competence and willingness, she had volunteered to go into "the field" at Warrenton.

By the time Walker arrived at Warrenton, conditions were horrible. She asked for permission to take the sickest patients to Washington for better care. Typhoid, a devastating disease caused by poor hygiene in the camps, on the battlefield, and in hospitals, wreaked havoc on the battle-weary. Symptoms included fever and loss of appetite, and victims fell in and out of consciousness for days. If their immune systems could not fight the disease, the bacteria made its way into the soldiers' small intestines and caused severe intestinal problems. Fevers spiked, produced internal bleeding, and weakened the pulse until almost all of the infected soldiers died.

There were more deaths from disease and wounds in the American Civil War than from bullets. Both the Confederate and Union armies suffered outbreaks of disabling conditions that sapped their fighting ability and drained resources. Diarrhea, caused by everything from food poisoning to parasites to infection, was so common that it was called "the soldier's disease." Military men who managed to find humor in the situation joked that they had learned to shoot from a squatting position. Malaria, smallpox, yellow fever, measles, and other infectious diseases spread through camps in waves.

Major General Ambrose E. Burnside issued an order that "Dr. Mary E. Walker be authorized to accompany and assist in caring for, from Warrenton Virginia to Washington, D.C., the sick and wounded soldiers now at the former post. The surgeon in Charge there will afford every facility to Dr. Walker for that purpose."

Before she could even move them, however, Walker had to care for their immediate needs. Sick men were lying on the floor of an old house, and the man in charge told Walker he was worn out. "For God's sake do something for them if you can," he said.

She began by searching for a washbasin. After going to several houses, she succeeded in buying a basin for one dollar from a woman whom she convinced could wash and cook vegetables in her only other remaining pot.

With the basin in hand, she hastened back to the sick men. The camp had few supplies, so she tore up one of her long nightgowns to make small square towels. She instructed one of the camp's healthy soldiers to wash the patients' faces and hands and then to pass out clean water. When word of her attempts to alleviate the suffering of her patients got out, many were scandalized that she had dared to expose a feminine undergarment.

Some people admired Walker's spirit and creativity, while others condemned her for stepping outside societal boundaries. She made little effort to understand or cater to the feelings of her detractors. This lack of finesse eventually hurt her causes, though during the war her accomplishments for the greater good generally outweighed her missteps.

On the train ride to Washington, Walker made sure that her patients were as comfortable as possible, despite the fact that there was little food, no medicine, and few blankets. She helped the least severely wounded to the top of the train cars, and the rest into six freight cars and one passenger car. She bathed feverish faces, cleaned wounds, and spoke encouragingly to the weak. When the train stopped suddenly in a desolate place, Walker discovered that one of the engineers had taken part of the train to Alexandria, Virginia. She realized that there was no one in the remaining cars who could order the engineer to continue to Washington, so she did it herself.

As Walker checked on her patients, she noticed one man near death. "I asked him his name, which I wrote down,

This woodcut shows wounded soldiers being loaded onto a train after the battle at Fair Oaks, Virginia. (Courtesy of North Wind Pictures)

but before I could get anything more except his regiment, he had passed to the beyond," she remarked.

Walker subsequently recorded the details of other soldiers she recognized as near death, and when they passed away, she wrote to their families, noting their courage and brave conduct. Years later, the father of one of the deceased soldiers used Walker's letter to claim his son's pension.

After she had cared for the soldiers suffering from typhoid and had overseen their transport to Washington, Walker was soon back in the field, this time at Fredericksburg, Virginia, where the Union army had suffered a painful defeat. General Burnside had made some serious errors as he prepared for his first major battle. During the battle, cannonballs and shells bombarded Fredericksburg and slammed through the windows, roofs, and walls of civilian homes. When the battle was over, nearly 13,000 Union soldiers lay

The Battle of Fredericksburg

More than 380 major engagements were fought across twenty-six states during the war. The war has been called by many different names over time: The War between the States, The Confederate War, The War for States' Rights, The War for Constitutional Liberty, The War against Slavery, The Southern Rebellion, and even The War to Suppress Yankee Arrogance. While these different names belie the various viewpoints held by people about the war, no one—North or South—can deny that it was one of the bloodiest and most taxing conflicts in U.S. history.

In November of 1862, the Union Army of the Potomac marched toward Fredericksburg, Virginia, under the command of General Ambrose E. Burnside. The army had turned back a Confederate invasion of the North during the single bloodiest day of fighting yet at a battle near Antietam Creek in Maryland in September. This was the first setback for Confederate General Robert E. Lee, and now the Union soldiers were determined to smash Lee's smaller force before winter and put an end to the war at last.

General Burnside gave his attack orders on December 11, 1862. The battle began with a furious artillery barrage against Confederate troops hunkered in on the high banks of the Rappahannock River. When the Union attack came, however, the Confederate forces were ready and slaughtered the blue-coated attackers as they tried to make their way up the steep bluff. Bullets sliced the air and men fell to the ground, dead and dying, while smoke rolled over the fields and surrounding hills. Soon the ground was covered with wounded and dead men from both sides. At one location called Marye's Hill the bodies lay three-deep.

When the battle was over the scene left behind was horrible almost beyond words. Wounded men screamed and begged for help. They moaned for water and cried out to their friends as the weary survivors listened to the wails and delirious babbling. There was little that could be done until the ambulances and stretchers advanced through the mist and flickering campfires to try and rescue the wounded men.

By the end of the war in 1865, at least 618,000 Americans died, a number exceeding the nation's loss in all other wars, from the American Revolution to Vietnam. What's more, a larger number died from disease rather than from a bullet. The Union suffered a little more than 110,000 battle deaths and some 250,000 deaths from disease, and the Confederates suffered 94,000 battle deaths and 164,000 from disease.

Fredericksburg was a particularly bloody battle. In the three days of fighting, in December 1862, more than 100,000 Union troops and 72,000 Confederate troops engaged. The Union suffered one of its worst defeats, with more than 13,000 casualties.

Jane Beal, a resident of Fredericksburg wrote later, "I was too old, and weary, and heartsick, to bear the sight of blood and carnage. . . . One or two of the servants came back and gave me awful accounts of the scene on the road, the Ambulances of wounded men, the piles of amputated limbs already collecting in the corners of the yards at Mrs. Wiet's and Mrs. Goodwin's."

Almost everyone agreed that the battlefield was no place for a woman. Piles of arms and legs were not a sight the fairer sex should see. However, Mary Edwards Walker cared little for society's expectations as she walked the Fredericksburg battlefield.

dead or wounded, while others were classified as missing.

Walker labored in a hastily set up tent hospital across the Rappahannock River from Fredericksburg. She noticed that stretcher-bearers laid patients headfirst on the riverbank prior to loading them on boats for Washington, and she disapproved. She intervened.

"There seemed no one to manage that part of it," said Walker. "I stood close to the edge of the water and as soon as they were close enough so I could order them I did so, directing them to immediately turn around and take them feet first. It is almost needless to say that . . . taking them down headfirst would have produced pains in the head if not serious congestion of the brain on such a warm day. "

In January 1863, Dr. Preston King, who was with Walker at Fredericksburg, sent an account of her work to Secretary of War Edwin Stanton. King asked Stanton to compensate Walker, both for her time and the money she had spent out of her own pocket for soldiers' relief. However, because no law provided for this sort of compensation, Walker received only her daily allotment of food and drink. She also would not return to the field until September of the next year, after the Battle of Chickamauga in Tennessee,

Edwin Stanton, U.S. secretary of war from 1862–1868, became known for his forceful and energetic methods. (Library of Congress)

but in the intervening months she was still working for the public good and for her favorite causes.

Back in Washington in late 1863, Walker saw a crowd on the east side of the Treasury building and asked a policeman if someone had been hurt. It turned out that a soldier's pregnant wife had fallen. The woman, who had been searching desperately for her husband, was transported to a police station. There was nowhere else to take her. Walker described the woman in her desperate situation:

> She stated that this was her first child and that she intended to ascertain her husband's condition and then immediately return to her home, but that she had walked until she was nearly dead, trying to get accommodation in a hotel and had failed. She had then made efforts and pleaded to be taken into some private house where she had money enough to pay her expenses, but that none would allow her to stop with them.

Some cities had "women's homes" where single women could find accommodations, but Washington did not. Police officers often assisted wives, mothers, and sisters looking for loved ones in the Capitol city, but their resources were limited. These women, most of whom had never traveled far from their homes or gone anywhere without the protection of a male escort, ended up wandering the streets or sleeping in parks or doorways.

Walker was outraged that there was no place in Washington to house the women. She wrote to the mayor and asked for his help in establishing a house for lost women and children. She started raising money by giving speeches, and within a week, she rented a house on Tenth Street, opposite Ford's Theatre, for forty dollars a month. Next, she went to General Edward R. S. Canby and requested old blankets, sheets, pillowcases, and furniture.

Once she established the home and hired a matron to run it, Walker threw her energies into helping the women find information about their husbands, brothers, and sons. With so many temporary and makeshift hospitals tucked in and around Washington, Georgetown, and Alexandria it was hard for anyone to find out which wounded man had gone where.

Walker asked General Daniel H. Rucker to let an ambulance and a driver report to her each day so she could take the women around to the hospitals to search for their loved

A line of ambulances and their drivers wait at Washington's Harewood Hospital.
(Library of Congress)

ones. She also contacted local newspapers and asked editors to issue a call for women to meet to form an association. Out of that meeting came the first women's home association in Washington, with Walker as president. She worked for the association as a medical officer and secretary, but eventually left the group and turned its operation over to several physicians' wives.

Though this work was not her primary goal, Walker may have felt that anything she did to help soldiers would eventually help her cause. Also, the break from war action also gave her a chance to earn a little money through private practice. Her energies were going in too many directions for the practice to be successful, however, and she had to battle prejudice.

She managed to keep herself afloat financially, although it was a struggle. Dr. Lydia Sayer Hasbrouck, editor of The Sybil, asked her readership to assist Walker so she could continue the fight for dress reform and other good works. There was no great outpouring of money in response to the plea, but between her savings, donations, and earnings from her practice, Walker was able to stay in Washington the best part of a year. Then, near the end of 1863, tired of her civilian enterprises and eager to get back to the front, she wrote to Secretary of War Stanton to make her boldest request yet.

five

THE SOLDIER'S FRIEND

The Civil War was fought on several fronts. Throughout most of 1862, fierce fighting raged up and down the Mississippi River and surrounding countryside until it was brought under Union control. By September 1863 the central Mississippi Valley was under Union control, and its forces had advanced to Chattanooga, Tennessee. At Chickamauga Creek, Union and Confederate armies engaged. The result was a decisive victory for the North that pushed the Confederates out of the area and confined them to the states along the east coast. Chickamauga had been a bloody battle, though, and more than 7,000 wounded Union soldiers poured in from the battlefield.

Walker's restlessness brought her to the Tennessee front just after the battle. This time she came with a letter from Assistant Surgeon General R. C. Wood, who had wanted to give her a position after Surgeon General Finley turned her down at the Patent Office.

Though she offered both skill and experience, Walker had her usual trouble with the surgeon-in-charge at Chickamauga. He only wanted to use her as a nurse, but Walker's skills were too desperately needed for him to turn her away. Her talent and dedication soon caught the attention of Major General George H. Thomas, then in command of the Army of the Cumberland and known as "the Rock of Chickamauga." But Walker wanted to attract the attention

The Battle at Chickamauga Creek was one of the few where Union forces were outnumbered on the field. It would have been a decisive Confederate win had it not been for the bravery of Major General Thomas, Mary Walker's influential patron. (Library of Congress)

of someone who could give her a commission as she continued to push for some kind of formal place in the Union army. In November 1863, she wrote directly to Secretary of War Stanton. "Will you give me authority to get up a regiment of men, to be called Walker's U. S. Patriots, subject to all general orders, in Vol. Regts. [Volunteer Regiments]?" she wrote. "I would like the authority to enlist them in any loyal states. And also authority to tell them that I will act as first Assistant Surgeon."

She should have known that no one in the military would give her such authority, but she hoped that her fame as "the friend of soldiers" would make it more acceptable. She was wrong, as she often was in gauging the reaction to her breach of social mores. Stanton turned down her request.

Frustrated but undeterred, Walker wrote to President Abraham Lincoln in January 1864. In the letter, she asked for a commission and stated that she would prefer a battlefield assignment, where her "energy, enthusiasm, professional abilities and patriotism will be of the greatest service in inspiring the true soldier never to yield to traitors, and in attending the wounded brave."

Less than a week later, she received her reply: "The Medical Department of the Army is an organized system in the hands of men supposed to be learned in that profession, and I am sure it would injure the service for me, with strong hand, to thrust among them anyone, male or female, without their consent," Lincoln wrote.

However, because of a letter of recommendation from Congressman John Farnsworth of Illinois on Walker's behalf, Dr. Wood of the War Department sent Walker to Chattanooga for an evaluation of her qualifications by a medical board at the Department of the Cumberland. Walker appeared before this board of doctors on March 8, 1864. All assistant surgeons had to go through this process, but in such desperate times, the board was often just a formality. The medical director of the army of the Cumberland convened Walker's board, and the five men on the board made no effort to hide their hostility toward her. Board member Dr. George E. Cooper expressed his complete disdain for the idea of female surgeons. Another board member, Roberts Bartholow, called Walker a

The staff of the U.S. Medical Department line up in front of their Washington, D.C., headquarters. (Library of Congress)

"medical monstrosity" and pointed to the "hybrid costume" she wore to illustrate his point.

In a letter written in 1865 to President Andrew Johnson, who took office after Abraham Lincoln's assassination, Walker recalled that she "felt that the examination was intended to be a *farce*, & *more than half* the time was consumed in questions regarding subjects that were *exclusively feminine* and had no sort of relation to the diseases and wounds of *soldiers*."

The five doctors on the board condemned her abilities in the strongest terms, stating that they doubted whether she had studied medicine. The examining doctors may have dismissed her skills simply because she was a woman, or because they did not think Syracuse Medical College was a "regular" medical school. Whatever the reason, they recommended she be hired as a nurse in a general hospital.

In making such an assessment, the board ignored the evidence Walker provided to them. Doctors who actually worked with her, such as J. N. Green and Preston King, knew she was competent. Major General Alexander McCook had also welcomed Walker's assistance in Tennessee, and the "Rock of Chickamauga" himself, Major General Thomas, had been impressed by her hard work.

In the end, the serious shortage of doctors eventually worked in Walker's favor. Because one of the assistant surgeons with the Fifty-Second Ohio Volunteer Infantry regiment died, Colonel Daniel McCook Jr., ignoring the board's findings, appointed Walker as a replacement. (During the American Civil War, at least fifteen members of the

Major General Alexander McDowell McCook. (Library of Congress)

McCook family fought for the North on the Union side, including brothers Colonel Dan McCook and Major General Alexander. The family of Ohioans came to be known as the "Fighting McCooks.") He had been impressed with her work after Chickamauga, and now Walker became a contract surgeon assigned to a regiment. This meant no commission or rank in the army but, finally, some pay. She would make eighty dollars per month instead of the one hundred to one hundred thirty dollars a male assistant surgeon was paid. Still, this was much more than other women serving in the war were making. Walker joined the Fifty-second Ohio at its winter camp at Gordon's Mills, Georgia in March 1864.

At this new location, Walker found that the troops there did not need her immediate attention, but Confederate civilians did. Even though the civilians were potential rebels, Colonel McCook granted Walker permission to attend to their medical needs.

The civilians welcomed her services, and she traveled to distant corners to care for her Southern patients, sometimes spending the night away from camp. On one occasion, a mother refused to allow Walker to sleep in the same room with her daughter, saying that she was convinced Walker was a man. When Walker inquired about how they had arrived at such a conclusion, the mother responded that she did not think a woman could know so much. To convince the mother and daughter that she was not a man, Walker allowed the woman to pull her hair to prove that the long tresses were not part of a disguise.

Walker treated fevers and various aches and pains, delivered babies, and acted as a country physician to the people surrounding General McCook's camp. She gained their confidence, so much so that they shared with her where they hid their food and supplies.

> Some of them who had no cellars dug a small pit under the floor of the house and put provisions down there, then they nailed the floor down so that searchers from either army would not be likely to believe that they had anything hid there. Some people hid some

of their provisions in their beds, keeping a watch to
see when anyone was coming and then being quietly
seated as though they had not any information of
the approach of soldiers.

Walker believed that her care of and connection to the
civilians around the camp helped undermine the community's
rebel inclinations. "There is no doubt that General McCook's
kindness . . . and my professional duties to these people
caused a great many of them to abandon their allegiance
to the confederacy," she later wrote.

Some evidence suggests that Walker may have worked
as a spy at Gordon's Mills. A message to Major General
Thomas in 1864 asked if Walker deserved any commen-
dation for her actions and "secret services." Her recommendation for the Medal of Honor reported that she often
traveled over enemy lines in pursuit of information, and
that generals had changed their plans after taking that
information into consideration.

Walker did not leave a record of what she did during
most of her time at Gordon's Mills. Her reminiscences in
Incidents Connected with the Army are primarily anecdotes
about her experiences, and her other personal writings do
not mention spying.

Initially, Walker traveled the countryside around Gordon's
Mills with two orderlies and two officers. However, once
she became familiar with the area, she made the rounds
alone, often unarmed.

Alone one day, Walker was on her way to extract some
teeth for a woman. Along the way, she met two men who

suspected that she was a spy for the Union army, based on her dress and speech. When Walker attempted to reach for her medical instruments to prove that she was a doctor—and not a spy—one of the men insisted she halt, possibly fearing that she might have been armed. After a time, the two let her pass. When Walker returned to camp, she told General McCook about the incident, and she later identified one of the men as Champ Ferguson, a notorious rebel who had vowed to kill every "bluecoat" he saw.

On April 10, 1864, Walker either took a wrong turn or simply had the bad luck to ride into territory patrolled by Confederates. A sentry stopped her. When she claimed that she was unarmed and delivering letters, he took her into custody. She spent the night in a nearby cabin, and the next day was handed over to Confederate General D. H. Hill. In turn, he sent her to his headquarters where she remained for a week.

After her initial fright, Walker either accepted the situation and made the best of it or tried to learn what she could about Confederate plans. Walker was cooperative, and because the South had a shortage of doctors, she was allowed to treat a few soldiers.

Even though she was an enemy prisoner, she was an enormous curiosity to the Confederates. Several people paid her visits, including doctors who were trying to discover if she really had the qualifications to be a doctor. Within a few days of her capture, however, Walker was put on a train to Richmond, Virginia, so military authorities could decide what to do with her.

News of her capture and journey from Georgia to Virginia, spread and curious spectators gathered at every stop to gawk at her. Some undoubtedly just wanted a glimpse of such an unusual woman, but others were eager to both gloat at her capture and mock her. In Richmond, Confederate Captain Benedict J. Semmes wrote in a letter that the sight of a female doctor in men's clothes amused the troops. The *Richmond Sentinel* was just as unkind, stating in its report on her arrival in Richmond that she was ugly, skinny, and aging. Though she had not been caught with any incriminating documents or other evidence of spying, her captors evidently believed she either was a spy or meant them harm. Mary Edwards Walker was now a prisoner of war.

six

PRISONER OF WAR

I n Richmond, Walker was held at a prison called Castle Thunder, which was actually a converted tobacco factory—not a regular army stockade. It was a dismal prison, established to hold inmates charged with committing crimes against the Confederacy.

Shortly after Walker's arrival at Castle Thunder, Brigadier General William M. Gardner, the administrator in charge of Walker's case, met with her to give her a "fatherly lecture." Walker did not know what the general wanted from her. She was exhausted, anxious, confused, and frightened. She broke down in tears as Gardner harangued her with his lectures about a woman's place. Gardner took this as a sign that he had impressed her with the wisdom of his views and helped her restore her womanhood. It is more likely that Walker simply gave way to the strain and uncertainty of her capture and released her tension by crying.

Although Gardner considered Walker's behavior un-feminine, he was kinder than many when he described her as "the most personable and gentlemanly looking young woman I ever saw," who showed evidence of "good birth and refinement as well as superior intellect." In contrast, The Richmond *Whig* ridiculed Walker as a monstrosity, an example of Yankee perversity.

The condemnation and insults of her captors were hard to take, but the physical hardship Walker endured was worse. Her prison mattress swarmed with bedbugs and fleas, and rats raced along the floors at night. Newspapers provided a covering for the filthy furniture, but she had nothing to mask the dirt and rank smells.

Despite her situation, Walker wrote to her parents, saying, "I hope you are not grieving about me because I am a prisoner of war. I am living in a three-story brick 'castle' with plenty to eat, and a clean bed to sleep in. I have a roommate, a young lady about twenty years of age from near Corinth, Mississippi . . . the officers are gentlemanly and kind, and it will not be long before I am exchanged. "

The letter masked the truth. A niece said later that her aunt received one meal a day, with the rice full of maggots and the bread moldy, and that she thought she would have died in prison if she had not been able to procure some eggs through a commissary clerk. Walker

Soldiers patrol the inner courtyard of Castle Thunder, the Confederate prison where Dr. Mary Walker was incarcerated for four months starting in April of 1864. (Library of Congress)

later claimed she weighed 105 pounds upon entering the prison and sixty when she left.

Conditions were miserable in southern prisons, and Castle Thunder was no exception. All over the South, supplies of even the barest necessities were low. Food, firewood, and clothing were either completely unavailable or obtainable only at the highest prices.

Confederate soldiers, generals, and prisoners alike all suffered from starvation. Even General Robert E. Lee, commander of the Confederate army of Northern Virginia, dined meagerly. The Mobile *Advertiser* recounted that his ordinary dinner consisted of a head of cabbage, boiled in salt water, and pone of cornbread. It was recorded that in Richmond, on May 15, 1864, bacon sold for nine dollars a pound, butter for fifteen dollars a pound, and a pair of chickens cost thirty dollars.

Boys and old men were being pressed into service, and civilians were near starvation. The Confederacy had little to offer its citizens, let alone burdensome prisoners. Of the nearly 200,000 Union detainees in Confederate prisons, more than 30,000 died in captivity, mainly due to shortages of supplies and medical care.

Castle Thunder had developed a brutal reputation. By this point in the war, prison guards and their overseers were men who could not be used in a more productive capacity elsewhere. Castle Thunder guards took random shots at prisoners' cells, and prisoners believed that sentries looked for an excuse to shoot and kill them.

Walker stood at her cell door one day and narrowly missed being struck by a bullet. The guard said it was an accident, but such accidents happened frequently. The prison had a whitewashed room with bars on the window, the only place prisoners could walk freely. Supposedly, there was also a "deathline" across which prisoners could not step or they would be shot dead.

Guards controlled the water supply, which prisoners could access only with the guards' approval. The air inside was stagnant and foul, and outdoor exercise was not allowed. Heat and humidity added to the dreadful conditions. Walker offered to treat the most severely wounded prisoners, but the authorities did not trust her and turned down her offer.

In these difficult circumstances, Walker continued to wear her pants-dress outfit and to defend it. A minister who had visited the prison wrote about her "Bloomer costume"

This girl wearing the short dress and pantaloons made popular by Amelia Bloomer is featured on the cover of "Bloomer Waltz: Costume for Summer" an 1851 musical piece by William Dessier. (Library of Congress)

in a local paper, and Walker wrote a letter to the editor of the paper to correct the reference to her clothing as "male attire." In the letter, she wrote "Sir: will you please correct the statement . . . in regard to my being 'dressed in male attire,' as such is not the case. Simple justice demands correction. I am attired in what is usually called the 'Bloomer' or 'Reform

Dress,' which is similar to all ladies with the exception of its being shorter and more physiological than long dresses."

Walker also made no secret about her desire to be set free and wrote letter after letter to anyone she thought could help. Nauseated by the poor food and weakened by her confinement, she still found the energy to wave a small United States flag as she sat near an open window to try to catch a breeze in the stifling heat.

Finally, on August 12, 1864, Walker and several hundred prisoners sailed to Fortress Monroe, which was in Virginia but behind Union lines. She had been at Castle Thunder four months. Walker always believed that she had been exchanged for a Confederate major, a great source of pride

The New York *sailed under a flag of truce because it returned exchanged prisoners to both sides. The boat brought Confederate prisoners, like Mary Walker, to Union-controlled Fortress Monroe.* (Library of Congress)

to her. In reality, she and twenty-four other Union doctors were exchanged for seventeen Confederate doctors.

Her contract as surgeon for the Fifty-Second Ohio expired just after her release from prison. After a quick trip to the Fifty-Second to gather her belongings, Walker returned to Washington. Her hometown paper, the *Oswego Commercial Times*, reported that she made the trip to "settle her business; obtain her trunk and bid adieu to the army. She will make a tour through the States and lecture on her experiences 'Down in Dixie.'"

Walker did visit the Fifty-second Ohio, but it was not to bid the army adieu. Instead, she wrote to Union commander Major General William Tecumseh Sherman.

> Having acted in various capacities, since the commencement of the rebellion, without a Commission from Government & three years of service having Expired, I now most respectfully ask that a Commission be given me, with the rank of Major, & that I be assigned to duty as surgeon of the female prisoners & the female refugees at Louisville Ky.

Her old ally Major General Thomas supported her request and asked that she receive the rank of major. His letter of endorsement still was not enough, but he did manage to help her in another way. On August 23, Thomas forwarded by telegraph a copy of Major General McCook's order assigning Walker to the Fifty-second Ohio. Thomas recommended that Walker be paid retroactively from March 11 to August 24, 1864, as a contract physician. Stanton approved the request, and the money—and legitimacy of her service—finally appeared.

Sometime in early September 1864, Walker received $432.36 for her services as a contract assistant surgeon. This payment was the first money she had received during her years of service to the Union army.

Her request for a commission was once again denied, but Walker did get another contract with the army. Her orders required her to act as a medical officer whenever she was needed to do so and to keep stock of surgical tools and instruments. In return, she would receive between one hundred dollars and $113.83 per month, depending on her actual duties, and transportation while performing service in the field. Army authorities also approved Walker's request for duty at the Louisville Female Military Prison, which primarily held Confederate women who were accused of spying or other anti-Union acts.

Finally, Walker had an assignment with official approval and authority. Her title was surgeon in charge. All that remained to be seen was how the prisoners and those in authority would react to her appointment.

seven

PRISON DOCTOR

By the end of 1864 both the North and South were weary of fighting and dying. The once anticipated glory of battle had turned into a series of fearful names that broke the hearts of most of those who heard them: Antietam, Gettysburg, Vicksburg, Cold Harbor, and dozens of others. Union General William Tecumseh Sherman had begun a march across Georgia with the intention of ending the war by destroying the remaining infrastructure in the South and breaking the civilians' will to carry on with the war. The war had dramatically and profoundly changed the nation. Walker had changed as well.

Her physical health had declined during her imprisonment, and she knew it would be difficult to keep up with battlefield work. "The impossibility of obtaining sufficient food to properly sustain life, so injured my whole system as to make me incapable of practicing my profession,"

Walker later told a pension board. "My eyes have been severely injured. In the middle of August 1864, I could not read a dozen lines in an ordinary newspaper."

She arrived at the Louisville, Kentucky, hospital prison in October 1864 as the surgeon-in-charge. Her captivity would help her to empathize with the plight of prisoners. However, medical duty at a women's prison would bring none of the recognition she had received for her battlefield duty. Also, the doctor who had been in charge of both the men and women in the Louisville prison before her arrival was unwilling to give up his oversight of the female prisoners. Dr. E. O. Brown had been forced to step aside as supervisor of the women's prison because of Walker's assignment. Now he only supervised the male prison. He considered it a demotion. Brown, and other doctors before him, had managed the prison so poorly that the place had acquired a dreadful reputation. Brown, for example, had allowed the women great freedom during his tenure, and they had taken advantage of it. They were over-friendly with the guards and other visitors to the point that there was suspicion of prostitution. They sang rebel songs, spoke badly of the Union, and were habitually dirty and rude. Post Commander Lieutenant Colonel J. H. Hammond wrote to Colonel R. C. Wood comparing the women's prison to a brothel. Hammond continued, saying that he was sure Walker's arrival would bring improvement.

Within two weeks of Walker's arrival, Dr. Brown wrote a letter of complaint to Colonel Wood: "I regard Dr. M. E. Walker as incompetent to prescribe for the sick in the

The small pin on Walker's left shoulder reads, "Extra Assistant Surgeon, Army of the Potomac, War of 1861." (Courtesy of Oswego County Historical Society)

Female Prison, and would further state that her tyrannical conduct has been intolerable not only to the inmates of the Prison, but to myself."

Brown wasted no time in trying to undermine her, but Walker did not hesitate to try and outmaneuver him. She contacted Hammond to ask that he keep Brown from interfering with her, to take measures to ensure her authority, and to prevent Brown from visiting the Female Military Prison to encourage the inmates to disobey her orders.

Walker needed Hammond's support. Besides being a newcomer, she faced a number of challenges. Brown was openly and actively hostile to every change Walker tried to make, and although he no longer ran the Female Prison Hospital, he retained influence.

Other males in authority did not hesitate to display their animosity as well. An affidavit, a written declaration made under oath, from one of Walker's orderlies, Cary C. Conklin, says "The Lieut. commanding the guard seemed to take every opportunity, and study to do whatever he thought would annoy and make the position of the Surgeon in Charge [Walker] a very trying one."

On one occasion, when Walker took a prisoner out of the building for a walk, the same lieutenant challenged her right to do so. He sent Walker and the prisoner under guard to Edward E. Phelps, the Army Post's medical director. Phelps dismissed the women, sent the guards back, and gave the lieutenant a piece of his mind. "You have no business to interfere with the Medical Dept. of the Prison," he said. "And further, if the Officer in Charge of that Dept. chooses to take her patients to *Canada* you should not in any way interfere in her business, as she alone is responsible." The support Walker received from Phelps and Hammond was the only reward for her efforts.

Walker launched into her duties as she understood them—to upgrade the physical and moral well-being of her charges—with vigor. She attempted to establish new rules in the women's prison, emphasizing cleanliness, and she tried to curtail the women's unruly behavior, especially around the young children imprisoned with their mothers. She watched over the interaction between the inmates and visitors, and stopped disloyal talk. Walker found the prisoners diet of soup, potatoes, fresh beef, and bread almost luxurious compared to the conditions she endured in a Confederate prison.

Within a month of her arrival, the female prisoners sent a letter to Colonel Fairleigh, the commander of the Twenty-sixth Kentucky Volunteers, asking him to replace Walker. They specifically requested Dr. Brown as her successor, saying they knew and liked him. Fairleigh sent the prisoners' letter on to Dr. Wood, who would still not oppose Major General Sherman's original request that Walker work at the prison.

Wood, like Hammond, supported Walker. However, someone less supportive and sympathetic to her soon replaced Hammond. Walker quickly found herself under fire. In January 1865 she sent the new post commander, Lieutenant Colonel Coyle, an angry letter of defense: "I thought you a man of sufficient discretion and judgment to comprehend things as they exist," Walker began. She then summed up the complaints against her:

> First I would not allow rebel songs and disloyal talk. The Lieut, would say 'O they are women.' Second, I would not allow familiarity between the Guards, male cooks and Prisoners. Third, all four of the male cooks were relieved and females supplied in their places, by the direction of Col Fairleigh. Fourth, I exacted cleanliness. Fifth, I would not allow prisoners to abuse each other. Sixth, I would not allow them to neglect their small children or abuse them.

Walker explained that her actions were intended to counteract the behavior of the prisoners. She ended her letter by saying that her superiors had always had confidence in her abilities. Within a few days, Walker received orders to confine her work solely to medical affairs. Ironically, it was the first time she had been ordered to serve as a doctor.

By March of 1865, six months after being assigned to the Female Military Prison, Walker had begun to wear down. She had not recovered fully from her own imprisonment. She was also living with the active disdain and hostility of almost everyone with whom she had daily contact and struggling with problems others had created. She tried to fight her enemies, but her assertiveness, stubbornness, and tenacity only made the situation worse.

Despite her best efforts, Walker grew increasingly weary of the tasks before her and requested a transfer. Edward Phelps, who admired Walker, released her from duty at the prison. She then requested a surgeon's position at the front. Instead, she was transferred to an orphans' asylum and refuge home in Clarksville, Tennessee, where she worked until the end of the war in April 1865.

On April 9, 1865, Confederate General Robert E. Lee surrendered to Union General Ulysses S. Grant at Appomattox, Virginia. It was Easter Week. On Good Friday, April 14, Lincoln was assassinated as he attended a play at Ford's Theater, across the street from the home set up by Walker for destitute women in Washington. By the next morning, Lincoln was dead.

Mathew Brady, a renowned Civil War photographer, convinced Robert E. Lee to sit for a photo shoot on the porch of his Richmond, Virginia, home soon after his surrender at Appomattox. (Library of Congress)

Walker's release from service in Clarksville ended unceremoniously with a letter from one of her most vocal critics in the Medical Department, Dr. George Cooper: "Madam, I am informed that your services are not needed at the Refugee home in Clarksville, Tenn., inasmuch as the Medical Officer in Charge can do all the work required of him. You can present yourself at either this office or that of the Asst Surgeon General as your services are no longer required in this Dept. "

It was clearly time for a new beginning. Walker needed to decide how she would use the notoriety gained both as a surgeon to the Union army and as a writer on topics such as dress reform and women's suffrage.

One thing was certain: her new beginning had to involve a job. From October 1861 to June 1865, Walker had received only $766.16 for her services to the Union army. She departed the service run-down, weary of thankless tasks, suffering from poor eyesight, and nearly broke. Unattached, but not yet hopeless, Walker returned to Washington.

eight

MEDAL OF HONOR

Walker decided to petition for a commission in the peacetime army. With her wartime service, prisoner of war status, and support from powerful generals, she hoped to finally achieve in peacetime what had eluded her during the war.

She asked for an appointment as a medical inspector at the Bureau of Refugees, Freedmen and Abandoned Lands. After the war, during the Reconstruction period, Congress established the bureau to provide practical, day-to-day aid to four million newly free slaves and impoverished whites. It was a shrewd tactic to ask for this position rather than a more mainstream surgeon's post. She did not expect the same kind of resistance from military authorities for such a position.

She wrote directly to President Andrew Johnson. Many of her friends with influence in the military also wrote to Johnson on her behalf, extolling her character and achievements during the war.

President Johnson was impressed by these and other letters and asked Secretary of War Stanton if he could give Walker a commission. Stanton replied that giving her the commission and title of surgeon was "novel in character" but could be done. Stanton left the final decision to the new surgeon general, M. B. Ames, who was not in favor of it. Ames said that the medical board of examiners had found Walker's training not up to army standards, and he also noted that there was no law or regulation that would allow the commission.

Walker knew that she had to keep her name and petitions in front of the proper authorities if she wanted a commission. In September 1865 she sent President Johnson a long report detailing her experience in the military and defending her reputation.

In October, she pushed for a brevet promotion to major. A brevet promotion was a commission granted as an honor, which promoted a military person without an increase in pay or authority. A brevet could not be awarded without a prior commission, though. The matter was referred to Lieutenant General Ulysses S. Grant, who said that it would not be proper to give a military commission to a female.

President Johnson finally asked Judge Advocate General J. Holt of the War Department's Bureau of Military Justice if Walker could receive an appointment in the medical department of the army. Holt wrote a twelve-page reply to the president in which he pointed out that Walker's request for a commission was primarily a request for formal acknowledgment of her services. Walker and her supporters had actually petitioned for a commission that would be retroactive to her service at the Female Military Prison in Louisville. She had promised to re-sign the commission if it were granted. Holt agreed with Surgeon General Ames that there was little precedent for a commission but did not actually say there was a legal obstruction to it.

Holt then discussed Walker's gender. He acknowledged that government departments other than the War Department had previously selected women for public offices of trust and importance. He suggested that the focus should be on Walker's merits.

Holt reviewed letters and testimonials from doctors who had served with Walker. He looked at documents that established her credentials and at military documents that confirmed her skill and competency in carrying out the assignments she had received. He concluded by examining written records concerning her imprisonment.

Holt concluded with disappointing news: in spite of the evidence of her service, she was to be denied her request because she had not completed all the requirements of an army doctor.

He added, though, that there was nothing to rule out a reward in the form of some recognition for Walker's services on behalf of the Union.

Walker's Citation

Mary Walker's citation was an unusually long one, especially as most were only a few lines. Her entire Medal of Honor reads:

Whereas it appears from official records that Dr. Mary E. Walker, a graduate of medicine, "has rendered valuable service to the Government, and her efforts have been earnest and untiring in a variety of ways," and that she was assigned to duty and served as an assistant surgeon in charge of female prisoners at Louisville, Ky., upon the recommendation of Major-Generals Sherman and Thomas, and faithfully served as contract surgeon in the service of the United States, and has devoted herself with much patriotic zeal to the sick and wounded soldiers, both in the field and hospitals, to the detriment of her own health, and has endured hardships as a prisoner of war for four months in a southern prison while acting as a contract surgeon; and Whereas by reason of her not being a commissioned officer in the military services a brevet or honorary rank can not, under existing law, be conferred upon her; and Whereas in the opinion of the President an honorable recognition of her services and sufferings should be made; *It is ordered.* That a testimonial thereof shall be hereby made and given to the said Dr. Mary E. Walker, and that the usual medal of honor for meritorious services be given her.

"Given under my hand in the city of Washington, D.C., this 11th day of November, A. D. 1865. "

ANDREW JOHNSON,
President

President Johnson, along with two of Walker's staunchest supporters, Major General William Tecumseh Sherman and Major General George H. Thomas, wanted to recognize Walker for her services. The two generals recommended her for a medal, and on November 11, 1865, President Johnson signed a bill to present Walker with the Congressional Medal of Honor for Meritorious Service.

Dr. Mary Walker's Congressional Medal of Honor. (Courtesy of Oswego County Historical Society)

With Johnson's recommendation, Walker became the first woman to win the Congressional Medal of Honor, an award established by Congress to honor those who served the Union army with distinction. Walker had finally achieved recognition for the assistance she had provided to the Union cause. A military career was definitely closed to her, however, and she decided to pursue other interests.

Walker began to lecture on dress reform, health, and temperance issues. She was concerned that women continued to wear clothing that was not practical or healthy. Crinoline cages and other kinds of hoop skirts were still popular, although the war had shown that they were not always functional. Women working in army camps learned quickly that hoop skirts were hard to control and could easily catch fire when worn around flames. Although most women continued to wear traditional, long skirts even on duty as nurses or cooks, many abandoned the cumbersome cages that hampered their movements.

Shortly after the war, Walker was elected president of the National Dress Reform Association. In her first speech to the group, Walker offered a prediction: "Women will have equal rights with men within ten years." She also showed her wry sense of humor: "I know a fitting punishment for (ex-Confederate) President Jefferson Davis," she began. "Treat him like a woman! He should be forced to wear hoop skirts and a tight corset, and do housework in a four-story home. This," Walker claimed, "would be a worse punishment than any prison term."

Although well known for her stand on dress reform, Walker also vehemently opposed liquor and tobacco use. During the war, she witnessed countless episodes of drunkenness or alcohol abuse, as well as tobacco chewing and smoking.

"Tobacco cannot be used in any form, without producing evil effects, mentally or physically, sooner or later, upon the user, the wife, and the children," Walker said. She insisted that many physical ailments resulted from tobacco and alcohol, including insanity and paralysis.

Her lectures and speeches went over well, and in the summer of 1866, she was named a delegate to a Woman's Social Science Convention in Manchester, England. At the convention, Walker made a rousing speech about women's suffrage. She wore her usual attire, and her speech and appearance made headlines in the British newspapers. Soon she received other invitations to speak.

Walker began to realize that she was a bit of a celebrity and that people would pay to hear her speak. She had been living on meager wages for a long time and now saw a way to earn the money she needed and advance the causes she loved.

nine

LECTURE
CIRCUIT

Walker often faced physical danger during the American Civil War, but public speaking required a different sort of bravery. She risked speaking to audiences that might not be sympathetic to causes she supported, or even courteous.

On November 20, 1866, she gave a speech at St. James Hall in London to a paying audience. An advertisement announced her topic: "The Experiences of a Female Physician in College, in Private Practice and in the Federal Army." She spoke for ninety minutes about her experiences in medical school and on the battlefield. During the speech, she endured an audience of hissing men who stamped their feet, booed, hooted, and made kissing noises. Walker ignored the disruption and finished her speech.

*Walker had this portrait
taken on her speaking tour in
London.* (Courtesy of Oswego
County Historical Society)

Newspaper coverage characterized the speech as inter-
esting and described Walker's voice as clear and eloquent,
and her face as calm and pretty. The newspapers also
denounced those who disrupted the lecture, referring to
them as a mob.

As always, medical professionals were not so kind. One
medical journal said that Walker's opening remarks at St.
James were "as prosy as anything we had the ill fortune
to hear in our student days." It went on, saying that Walker's
talk did little more than "to throw ridicule on herself,
her sex, her profession, and her country, and to strengthen

the opinions of those who hold that women had better not meddle in physics."

Other medical journals were just as unkind, with one calling her the "American Medical Nondescript." Their jabs were repeated in American medical journals. One reviewer even published a letter from Dr. Roberts Bartholow, a member of the medical board at Chattanooga that had questioned Walker's medical skills, suggesting that Walker had no more medical knowledge than the common housewife.

Although the medical community had not admired her speech, Walker gave a large number of speeches in the following months on topics including dress reform and her war experiences to audiences across England and Scotland.

Despite her hard work and the large crowds she attracted, Walker never earned much money as a lecturer. She spoke for free to the poor and to children, and only charged her paying audiences enough to cover her expenses. All her life, Walker never managed to prosper from her experiences—she got by, but just barely. She returned from England with financial need pressing upon her.

Walker may have grown used to her celebrity status in England, but she soon discovered that the citizens of Washington, D.C., were far less interested in her than the British had been.

She was scarcely able to make a living and was soon asking her congressman to introduce a bill in Congress granting her a pension. She maintained that her imprisonment in Castle Thunder had weakened her eyes to the point that she could not support herself. She wanted a disability pension for her service, such as many males received after being wounded. Her request was denied, and she set about organizing a speaking tour to raise money.

Walker traveled first across New England and then embarked on a longer tour across the country. Her passion for improving the lives of women, whether through dress reform, voting rights, or better treatment from their

The 1871 edition of Mary Walker's book Hit *included an engraving of Walker and her signature,* Mary E. Walker, M.D. (Courtesy of Oswego County Historical Society)

male counterparts, had never dimmed.

In December of 1869, she received an invitation from a woman named Mary Reed to come to Mississippi for a speaking engagement. Walker wrote back to accept the invitation. She added in closing: "My heart is filled with *more than regard* for the Southern Sisterhood, for you like us, must feel the degradation of all unenfranchised women in a *professed to be* Republican country."

Walker then hurried to Mississippi only to find that the invitation had been a hoax and that Mary Reed did not exist. She had been promised a speaking engagement and a fee that would not be forthcoming.

The hoax was one in a series of insults that Walker suffered in her career. Long-held views about women's roles proved hard to change. The country had accepted significant exceptions to a woman's place in society during the Civil War—such as allowing women to work as nurses and run the family farm—but many men, and women too, wanted to return to "normal" life after the war. Wives and daughters were relieved to be free of all the chores and double-duty they had performed during the war years. They also longed for fashionable clothes and other niceties. To the despair of dress reformers like Walker, women began eagerly purchasing fashions from Paris and Great Britain.

Ever determined, Walker continued her crusade. "It is not only *silly* that an immortal mind should be absorbed for half a lifetime, on fashionable follies . . . but it is a *sinful waste of time and energies*," she wrote. "A woman expends more vitality in wearing such a Dress, than a horse does wearing his harness, even if it were not removed except to curry and bathe him."

Voting rights was another key issue for Walker. She argued passionately against the injustices of women. She also protested against the use of tobacco and alcohol, calling them poisons that ruined both the user and his family. Finally, she urged both men and women to change their attitudes about work. Women's work was valuable, she declared. *All* work was valuable. She wanted to see men get the training they needed so they could enjoy good jobs and women to be paid what their work was worth.

Few people disagreed with everything Walker said, so she found audiences wherever she went. But she also attracted controversy. At one point a policeman arrested her in New York for wearing men's clothing. He took her to the police station, where he had to listen to a spirited lecture on dress reform. His superiors ordered Walker's release and made sure she was not arrested again in New York. That did not help her in Kansas City, where she also had a chance to lecture an unfortunate policeman who made the mistake of arresting her.

Walker attracted paying audiences to her speeches, but expenses were high and she ended up with little money. She decided to complete a book that she had been working on, *Hit*, which contained many of her thoughts on dress reform, the rights of women, alcohol and tobacco use, and marriage. The book was published in 1871, and between book sales, speeches, and a few patients, Walker earned enough to live on.

Lecturing and touring proved hard work, especially given the transportation of the time. Walker could not maintain a medical practice that would sustain her, although she continued to see patients on and off for almost all of her life. Her sisters and brother had their own families to care for, and she was too independent to want to live in Oswego on the charity of a family member. She was growing older and tired but was too poor to stop. Mary Walker had no choice but to keep fighting.

HIT

ESSAYS ON
WOMEN'S RIGHTS

MARY E.
WALKER, M.D.

WITH AN INTRODUCTION BY
MERCEDES GRAF

CLASSICS IN WOMEN'S STUDIES

Walker's book Hit *was reissued in 2003.*

ten

Continuing Disappointments

Walker's life experiences had taught her that her work was undervalued. As she grew older and had still not been granted a pension, she continued searching for a way to earn a living. In 1871, she considered taking a government job, which was one of the few sectors in the economy in which women could earn good salaries. Francis E. Spinner, the treasurer of the United States, recommended her as a temporary clerk in the Treasury. Walker applied for the position, passed the required examination, and took the oath of office. She showed up for work every day for two years, but she was never given a job to do.

Walker petitioned Congress for a payment of nine hundred dollars, which was equal to one year's salary. Several investigations were held, but Walker never received any money. Ultimately, a Congressional investigation into the matter found that the lack of payment probably had something to do with Walker's odd way of dressing and acting.

Walker's experience with the Treasury Department underscored how difficult it could be for a woman to make a living. She asked Congress for ten thousand dollars as compensation for her services during the war. She found, however, that war fever had died down considerably, and there was no rush to help those who had served in the Civil War.

Seven years had passed since Confederate General Robert E. Lee surrendered to Union General Ulysses S. Grant, ending the Civil War and marking the defeat of the Confederate forces. As the horrors of war faded, members of Congress had plenty of other issues on their minds, as the country expanded and recovered from the recent conflict. Many of the members were not familiar with Walker's record, and the bill asking for her relief went nowhere.

Walker did not give up. Her capacity for argument and perseverance were valuable tools, and her entreaties to Congress almost legendary—she petitioned at least twenty-five times for financial relief to the House, the Senate, or both. She gained one small victory in 1874 when Congress granted her a typical 50 percent disability pension of $8.50 a month for her eye injury. Even for those times, the sum was hardly enough. Widows who had not actually participated in the war received close to fifty dollars a month.

Civil War widows receive their pensions at the Sub-Treasury in New York City.
(Library of Congress)

Ironically, the Pension Office denied one request for an increase because "your appointment as such contract surgeon was made for the purpose . . . that you might be captured by the enemy to enable you to obtain information concerning their military affairs." This statement almost conceded that Walker had worked for the government as a spy. However, its conclusion was that when Walker was captured, she was not performing military duties as an assistant surgeon and was therefore not eligible for a pension.

When the Pension Office again reviewed Walker's request for an increase, a letter from the Surgeon General was produced to verify her service. This time the Pension Office said, "The records showed that her assignment to duty was in capacity of nurse, and not until her release from captivity was her appointment . . . as contract surgeon [given] to cover the time she was a prisoner of war."

Walker was infuriated. All of her life she had battled for recognition as a doctor. No one who knew her could possibly believe she would have accepted an assignment as anything other than a physician. She responded, "This is false as I never had a position as 'nurse' and would not accept one as either nurse or bootlick any more than would any other officer." To add insult to injury, the Pension Office turned her down again, not even granting her the twelve-dollar-a-month pension nurses received.

Walker continued to badger the government for an increase, saying she was determined to live long enough to obtain justice. Over time, she asked for ten thousand, two thousand, and then fifty dollars a month. She saw the request reduced to twenty-five dollars a month, and finally received twenty dollars a month in 1898, thirty-three years after the Civil War ended.

During the years of her pursuit of a government pension for her Civil War service, Walker did not neglect the cause of women's rights. She and many others—including some men—thought that women should be able to vote, own property, borrow money, work at an occupation for fair pay, get a divorce, and enjoy other rights that men took for granted. Walker complained that "You tax women and deprive them of the right of franchise . . . you imprison women for crimes you have forbidden women to legislate upon. The law does not say that women *shan't* vote."

Susan B. Anthony's quote "Failure is Impossible" became a rallying cry of the woman's suffrage movement. (Library of Congress)

Some women risked mockery, fines, and jail time to make their point. The tireless suffragette Susan B. Anthony and nearly fifty other women registered to vote in Rochester, New York, in 1871. On Election Day, Anthony and more than a dozen female supporters actually managed to cast ballots, and they were arrested for it. Anthony was found guilty at trial and fined one hundred dollars, but she refused to pay. To this day, the fine remains unpaid.

Walker believed that consistently going to the polls in large groups would eventually bring women the vote. Most other suffragettes grew tired of this method and believed that only a Constitutional Amendment would solve the problem. Walker adamantly opposed such a push—she believed the Constitution's language already gave women the vote. "I am opposed to granting men the right to vote on the *rights* of women," she said. She believed that if women needed to change anything, they should force each state to take out language in existing laws that restricted women's voting rights.

Walker wrote *The Crowning Constitutional Argument—The Opener of The Door For Women's Votes* as an authoritative statement of her position. One of her points in this essay is that the writers of the Constitution had exceeded their rights when they used the word "male" as a qualification for voting. Another point was that males had never been given the authority in that document to decide whether females could vote.

Her points may have been valid, but the more practical suffragettes did not see things Walker's way. They thought that putting the right words into the Constitution through an amendment would resolve their problem more quickly and easily than insisting on a new interpretation of the existing wording.

Despite these differences with her fellow suffragettes, Walker was effective in publicizing the unfairness of voting restrictions. An encouraging letter from a man named Preston Day likened Walker to a "seed sower" who must not get discouraged "because . . . the seed you sow is concealed in the cold, dark dirty ground where snakes, worms and toads crawl slimily."

The National Women's Suffrage Association and affiliated groups found it increasingly hard to work with Walker and eventually excluded her from their conventions. By the time she was in her fifties, Walker had managed to get on the wrong side of nearly everyone she worked with. Unfortunately, she still had to earn a living, and the abrasiveness of her personality finally began to tell against her.

eleven

RETURN TO OSWEGO

The 1870s were a particularly difficult decade for Walker. She had no steady employment. Her father had deeded the family farm to her in 1877 for one thousand dollars—money she had to scramble to find—but he retained a life interest in it. Her mother was allowed half the profits from the farm while she lived, leaving little for Walker herself even after her father died.

Her financial difficulties did not keep Walker from writing, and in 1878 she published another book. *Unmasked, or The Science of Immorality* was a sort of sex-and-marriage education manual for men. This book and her continued work for the suffrage movement created enough publicity for her to continue lecturing.

Walker received further publicity when she announced her candidacy for the United States Senate in 1881. Though she claimed to have a sharp mind, unharmed by any exposure to tobacco or alcohol, her election bid was not successful, and she pressed for a job with the federal government.

In May 1882, when she was almost fifty years old, Walker finally got a position as a clerk in the mailroom of the Pensions Office. She began well, recalling later that she was often approached to "give prescriptions and loan small sums of money, and do little offices of kindness that I *invariably* responded to." She launched into the job with enthusiasm and claimed to have come up with a postcard receipt system for registered letters, though this does not seem to be true. Although they do not name the person who thought it up, Post Office Department records show that the system was adopted in 1879, three years before Walker went to work in the mailroom. She also claimed to have pushed for the law that allowed senders to place their return addresses on the outside wrappers of the packages they mailed. She is generally credited with this innovation, but there is little available evidence to support that claim.

Walker liked to be at the center of any situation and typically did far more than was required of her. This trait generated appreciation and gratitude from many people she helped over the years, but it was not appreciated at the Pensions Office. She investigated what she considered abuses and inefficiencies, probably taking time from her assigned duties to do it. After ten months, the mailroom staff had enough. The assistant to the chief of the mail room said Walker was "a firebrand, insulting to the ladies and inattentive to her duties as clerk, spending her time in writing private correspondence."

She took a lot of sick leave during that period, which probably created some animosity as well. Walker was absent 112 days (three months out of ten), and complained about the conditions of the office while she was there. The office gave her sick leave, due to expire July 17. They dismissed her from her job on July 13, 1883, and barred her from entering the office when she returned on July 17. She was out of a job again.

Walker turned to something at which she had been successful in the past: touring and speaking. Even though lectures were still a popular form of public enter-tainment, she could not command the large audiences she once had. This time theater groups and vaudeville-type organizations sponsored her. She appeared on programs that included entertainment acts such as famous murder reenactments and curiosities such as Mexican feather workers.

An advertisement for the Wonderland Theater featured Walker's topics for one week: "Curiosities of the Brain," "Human Electricity," "Causes of Unusual Persons," and "Beauties, Uses and Injuries of Tobacco," among others. Other featured acts on the advertisement were "The Witch of Wall Street," who could foretell the future, a dress-cut-ting demonstration, trained canaries and parrots, and a

On the back of this photo Walker wrote, "Mary E. Walker, M.D. Speaking in N.Y. City," and someone else added a note that the performance was her last platform speaking engagement. (Courtesy of Oswego County Historical Society)

reenactment of the birth of Aphrodite. All of this entertainment was available to audience members for ten cents.

The work paid as much as one hundred fifty dollars per week. If Walker had been able to work all year, the salary would have been seventy-eight hundred dollars—a large sum for that time. Lecturing gave few people steady employment, however, and Walker only managed to get by.

She had no other way to earn a living, though. Her eyes were weak and she was physically frail. She had never found many steady patients as a physician, even when she still had the stamina to practice. Eventually Walker moved home to the farm outside of Oswego, New York, on which she had been born.

On the Oswego farm, Walker cared for her elderly mother, but she was absent so often that her mother moved in with Walker's brother, Alvah. In turn, he stabled his horses in Mary's barn, perhaps for the convenience, and perhaps because he felt she owed him something. Walker turned the horses loose.

Walker alienated many people with her views and actions, but one remained faithful, her sister Aurora. Aurora made sure Walker had food in the house when she came back from a trip, and she frequently tied up Walker's loose ends when she made abrupt departures.

In her will, Aurora wrote: "To my sister, Mary E. Walker, M. D., who is the poorest of my sisters, [I leave] my bay horse Barney, harness and red horse blanket . . . and all she owes me is canceled in consideration of her help in sickness and health."

As Walker grew older, she tried unsuccessfully to make a living from her farm. She tended a garden and sold the extra produce in town, but she had to mortgage her property to two brothers-in-law. Near the end of Walker's life, several concerned Oswego residents wrote to the town board on her behalf: "Gentlemen, we hereby petition your honorable body to set apart the sum of five hundred dollars for the assistance of Dr. Mary E. Walker as an indigent nurse of the Civil War living within our town limits whom the law compels the town to support."

Such indignities paled beside the insult Walker received in 1917, when Congress revoked her Medal of Honor. After the Civil War, the medal had been awarded to her under the original requirements. In 1916, Congress revised the Medal of Honor standards and reviewed past awards. The new law required "action involving actual combat with an enemy" and the recipient to have "distinguished himself conspicuously by gallantry or intrepidity, at the risk of his life, above, and beyond the call of duty." Also, each recipient had to have been discharged honorably from service.

This wording automatically excluded Walker, who had never received a military commission. The review board did allow some recipients to keep their medals in cases where evidence was missing and sometimes when "rewards which these men received were greater than would now be given for the same acts," but Walker's actions did not meet these requirements, and the board rescinded her medal.

Walker stubbornly refused to give up the medal. She argued that she had gone beyond enemy lines at the request of General Dan McCook at Gordon's Mills to treat civilians who lived in the area. Walker said, "I consider that my service at that time must be construed to be 'while in conflict' with the enemy [and] that it should come under the law in regard to the eligibility of the Medal of Honor people." She vowed to wear one of her medals—the original and a redesigned one from 1907—every day until she died. She did, and even though it was a misdemeanor offense to wear them, no one enforced the law in her case.

In 1917, Walker traveled to Washington, D.C., presumably to argue to have her medal restored. She was

An elderly Dr. Mary Walker in her customary top hat and overcoat. (Library of Congress)

eighty-five. There, she slipped on the Capitol steps, seriously injuring herself. She never fully recovered from the fall.

When she returned to Oswego, Walker paid off her debts and put her financial affairs in order. She set up her home almost as a museum, displaying mementos she had accumulated during her lifetime, along with furniture, photographs, and antiques.

Walker spent her last days with a neighbor, and in one of her last interviews, she recalled the excitement of her past: "Presidents and cabinet ministers and great generals were glad to meet and listen to me. . . . But now I am alone with the infirmities of age fast weighing me down and practically penniless, and no one wants to bother with me." She added philosophically, "Why should I complain?"

She died February 21, 1919, at the age of eighty-seven. By the time of her death, most people had forgotten who she was and the battles she had fought. Her household contents were sold at auction.

In many ways, Walker was far-sighted. Her stand against the dangers of tobacco and alcohol would find a receptive audience today, and she predicted a number of victories that would eventually empower women, including voting rights, more comfortable clothing, the availability of higher education, less restrictive divorce laws, and equal pay.

Some people accused her of being vulgar and chasing fame. Walker undoubtedly enjoyed the spotlight, but she never mentioned her war service in the two books she wrote. Any renown Walker attained was mixed with pain. She endured humiliation many times, along with the insults

This marker was placed by the Walker family in 1976 after the reinstatement of Dr. Mary Walker's Medal of Honor. (Courtesy of Oswego County Historical Society)

and scandalized comments of people who did not agree with her views.

Walker braved hostile countryside, battlefields, crude hospitals, and rowdy cities. She never flinched in approaching anyone she thought could help her or one of her causes. At Castle Thunder, she endured hunger, hostility, and filth.

Two of the social causes she championed, dress reform and women's suffrage, had met with some success by the time of her death. A bicycling fad in the late 1890s made a version of the Bloomer costume acceptable for women. World War I then opened occupations to women in which nonrestrictive clothing, including trousers, were allowed and preferred to long skirts. Women's suffrage had been granted in the Utah Territory in 1870, but its implementation in the United States would have to wait until shortly after Walker's death. The Nineteenth Amendment to the United States Constitution forbidding the denial of the vote on account of sex was passed by Congress in June 1919 and ratified by the states the next year.

Walker did not live to receive the personal vindication of the restoration of her Medal of Honor. One of her great grandnieces petitioned the Army Board of Corrections to reconsider the revocation of her great-aunt's award. The board ruled that the earlier board of 1916–1917 had made a mistake and U.S. president Jimmy Carter restored her Medal of Honor on June 11, 1977, with the following words:

> Although there is no one particular act of heroism, which is traditionally associated with the award of the Medal of Honor, there is ample evidence to show distinguished gallantry at the risk of life in the face of the enemy that the record shows the deceased was a prisoner of war for over four months; that she treated the wounded on the field of battle and went back and forth into enemy territory to administer to the sick and wounded of the military and civilian population; that such actions were of such a nature and also above and beyond the call of duty.

Dr. Mary Edwards Walker remains the only U.S. woman of the American Civil War, or any war, to have been awarded the honor. The U.S. Postal Service honored her with a twenty-cent first-class postage stamp in 1982.

Dr. Mary Edwards Walker, circa 1878. This is the earliest image of Walker wearing jacket, shirt and necktie. (Courtesy of Oswego County Historical Society)

Timeline

1832   Born November 26 in Oswego Town, New York.

1849   Elizabeth Blackwell becomes first woman in the U.S. to earn a medical diploma.

1850   Attends Falley Seminary in Fulton, New York.

1851   "Bloomers" make their appearance.

1853   Enters Syracuse Medical College in Syracuse, New York.

1855   Earns medical degree and begins practice in Columbus, Ohio.

1856   Marries Albert Miller; opens practice in Rome, New York.

1857   Begins writing to *The Sybil.*

1861   Civil War begins; Walker volunteers in Washington, D.C.

1862   Conducts wounded soldiers from Warrenton, VA, to Washington, D.C.

1863   Arrives in Tennessee after the Battle of Chickamauga.

1864   Meets medical board for pre-contract evaluation; captured and held prisoner at Castle Thunder, April–August.

1865	Civil War ends; receives Medal of Honor.
1866	Begins lecture tour in England.
1869	Receives divorce from Albert Miller; Wyoming extends the vote to women.
1870	Utah extends the vote to women.
1871	Publishes first book, *Hit;* tries unsuccessfully for job at the U.S. Treasury.
1874	Receives disability pension of $8.50 per month.
1878	Publishes second book, *Unmasked: The Science of Immorality*.
1881	Announces candidacy for U.S. Senate.
1882	Begins job at Pension Office.
1883	Dismissed from Pension Office.
1898	Receives increased pension of twenty dollars per month.
1907	Publishes *Crowning Constitutional Argument*.
1914	WWI begins.
1917	Medal of Honor is revoked; falls on Capitol steps; U.S. enters World War I.
1919	Dies February 21; 19th Amendment (women's right to vote) ratified on June 4.
1977	Medal of Honor is restored.
1982	U.S. Post Office issues a twenty-cent stamp honoring Dr. Mary Walker

Sources

CHAPTER ONE: Independent Spirit

p. 11, "her sex ought not to . . ." Mercedes Graf,
*A Woman of Honor: Dr. Mary E. Walker and the Civil
War* (Gettysburg, Pennsylvania: Thomas Publications,
2001), 34.

p. 18, "If hoops are worn, there . . ." Mary Edwards Walker,
Hit (New York: American News Co., 1871; repr. Amherst,
New York: Humanity Books, 2003), 84.

p. 18, "Resolved, That we can never . . ." *The Sybil*, 4, no.
24 (15 June 1860).

CHAPTER TWO: Rejecting Conventions

p. 25, "He told me that if . . ." L. J. Worden to Justice of
the Peace Doctor Grelmere, 21 March, 1866.

p. 25, "Nothing can make an individual . . ." Walker, *Hit*, 43.

p. 25, "To be deprived of a . . ." Ibid., 142

p. 26, "Those . . . who prefer . . ." *Rome Sentinel*, March 14,
1860.

p. 26, "I told him, and these were my words . . ." Africans in America, "Judgment Day: The Civil War," WGBH Educational Foundation, http://www.pbs.org/wgbh/aia/part4/4narr5.html (accessed 24 September 2006).

CHAPTER THREE: "I Cannot Appoint a Woman"

p. 33, "He stated that his . . ." Mary Edwards Walker, "Incidents Connected with the Army," 1799–1919. Mary Edwards Walker Papers, Syracuse University Library.

p. 33, "I cannot appoint a woman . . ." Elizabeth Leonard, *Yankee Women: Gender Battles in the Civil War* (New York: W. W. Norton & Company, 1994), 116.

p. 33, "I will work as your . . ." Walker, "Incidents Connected with the Army," Mary Edwards Walker Papers, Syracuse University Library.

p. 35-36, "No one knows who did . . ." Rebecca D. Larson, *White Roses: Stories of Civil War Nurses* (Gettysburg, Pennsylvania: Thomas Publications, 1997), 64.

p. 38-39, "I had assisted in an . . ." Walker, "Incidents Connected with the Army," Mary Edwards Walker Papers, Syracuse University Library.

p. 39, "I then made up my . . ." Ibid.

p. 39, "swear and declare . . ." Ibid.

p. 40, "I am assistant Physician . . ." Mary Edwards Walker to her brother and sister, 13 November, 1861.

CHAPTER FOUR: Working Without Pay

p. 47, "Dr. Mary E. Walker be . . ." Graf, *A Woman of Honor*, 32.

p. 47, "For God's sake do something . . ." Walker, "Incidents Connected with the Army," Mary Edwards Walker Papers, Syracuse University Library.

p. 48-49, "I asked him his name . . ." Ibid.

p. 51, "I was too old, and . . . " Jane Howison Beale, *Journal of Jane Howison Beale of Fredericksburg, Virginia, 1850–1862*, (1979): 75.

p. 51-52, "There seemed no one able . . ." Walker, "Incidents Connected with the Army," Mary Edwards Walker Papers, Syracuse University Library.

p. 53, "She stated that this . . ." Ibid.

CHAPTER FIVE: The Soldier's Friend

p. 58, "Will you give me authority . . ." Leonard, *Yankee Women*, 128.

p. 58, "energy, enthusiasm, professional abilities and . . ." Allen Mikaelian, *Medal of Honor: Profiles of America's Military Heroes from the Civil War to the Present* (New York: Hyperion, 2002), 7.

p. 58, "The Medical Department of the . . ." Charles Snyder, *Dr. Mary Walker: The Little Lady in Pants* (New York: Arno Press, 1974), 49.

p. 60, "felt that the examination . . ." Ibid., 131.

p. 62-63, "Some of them who had . . ." Walker, "Incidents Connected with the Army," Mary Edwards Walker Papers, Syracuse University Library.

p. 63, "There is no doubt that . . ." Ibid.

CHAPTER SIX: Prisoner of War

p. 67, "most personable and . . ." Graf, *A Woman of Honor*, 67.

p. 67, "I hope you are not . . ." Snyder, *Dr. Mary Walker*, 68.

p. 70, "Sir: will you please correct . . ." Ibid., 67.

p. 72, "settle her business . . ." Ibid., 47.
p. 72, "having acted in various capacities . . ." Leonard, *Yankee Women*, 141.

CHAPTER SEVEN: Prison Doctor

p. 74-75, "The impossibility of obtaining sufficient . . ." Graf, *A Woman of Honor,* 70.
p. 75-76, "I regard Dr. M. E. Walker as . . ." Leonard, *Yankee Women*, 143.
p. 77, "The Lieut. commanding the guard . . ." Mary Edwards Walker Papers, Syracuse University Library.
p. 77, "You have no business to . . ." Leonard, *Yankee Women*, 145.
p. 78, "I thought you a man . . ." Mary Edwards Walker to Commandant of Post, Louisville, Kentucky, 15 January 1865, in Mary Edwards Walker's Papers, Syracuse University Library.
p. 80-81, "Madam, I am informed that . . ." Leonard, *Yankee Women*, 149.

CHAPTER EIGHT: Medal of Honor

p. 87, "Women will have equal rights . . ." Mikaelian, *Medal of Honor*, 13.
p. 88, "Tobacco cannot be used . . . " Walker, *Hit*, 99.

CHAPTER NINE: Lecture Circuit

p. 90-91, "as prosy as anything we . . ." Snyder, *Dr. Mary Walker*, 70.

p. 92-93, "my heart is filled with . . ." Mary Edwards Walker to Mary L. Reed, 16 December 1869, in Mary Edwards Walker's Papers, Syracuse University Library.
p. 93, "it is not only silly . . ." Walker, *Hit*, 91.

CHAPTER TEN: Continuing Disappointments

p. 98, "your appointment as such contract . . ." Graf, *A Woman of Honor*, 66.
p. 98-99, "The records showed that her . . . " Ibid., 71.
p. 99, "This is false as I . . ." Ibid.
p. 99, " . . . you tax women and deprive . . ." Marlene Reckling Murty, *Mary Edwards Walker, M.D.* (Arlington, Virginia: The Women in Military Service for America Memorial Foundation, Inc., 1994), 4.
p. 101, "I am opposed to granting . . ." Snyder, *Dr. Mary Walker*, 103.
p. 102, "because . . . the seed you sow . . ." Preston Day to Mary Edwards Walker, 18 February 1873, in Mary Edwards Walker's Papers, Syracuse University Library.

CHAPTER ELEVEN: Return to Oswego

p. 104, "give prescriptions and loan small . . ." Snyder, *Dr. Mary Walker*, 115.
p. 105, "a firebrand, insulting to the . . . " Ibid., 115.
p. 107, "To my sister, Mary E. Walker, M. D. . . ." Ibid., 128.
p. 108, "Gentlemen, we hereby petition your . . ." John Stevenson, James M. Trosser, Simeon Stevenson,

and R. B. Hawley to the town board of the town of
Oswego N.Y., 1 October 1918, in Mary Edwards
Walker's Correspondence, Oswego County Historical
Society.

p. 108, "action involving . . . call of duty." Case Summary
for Mary Edwards Walker, Ref. File No. 13.9, ABCMR,
March 28, 1977.

p. 108-109, "I consider that my service . . ." Graf, *A Woman
of Honor,* 82.

p. 110, "Presidents and cabinet ministers and . . ." Snyder,
Dr. Mary Walker, 151.

Bibliography

Africans in America. "Judgment Day: The Civil War."
WGBH Educational Foundation. http://www.pbs.org/
wgbh/aia/part4/4narr5.html.

Beale, Jane Howison. *Journal of Jane Howison Beale of
Fredericksburg*, Virginia, 1850–1862. Fredericksburg,
VA: Historic Fredericksburg Foundation, 1995.

Commager, Henry Steele. *The Blue and The Gray*. New
York: The Fairfax Press, 1982.

Freemon, Frank R. *Gangrene and Glory: Medical Care
during the American Civil War*. Chicago: University of
Illinois Press, 1998.

Graf, Mercedes. *A Woman of Honor: Dr. Mary E. Walker and
the Civil War*. Gettysburg: Thomas Publications, 2001.

Groat, Charles V., PhD., Oswego Town Historian. *Dr. Mary
Walker: A Reader*. Oswego, 1994.

Jones, John Beauchamp. *A Rebel War Clerk's Diary, Vol.
II*. New York: Time-Life Books, 1982.

Larson, Rebecca D. *White Roses: Stories of Civil War Nurses.* Gettysburg: Thomas Publications, 1997.

Leech, Margaret. *Reveille in Washington 1860–1865.* New York: Harper & Brothers, 1941.

Leonard, Elizabeth D. *Yankee Women: Gender Battles in the Civil War.* New York: W. W. Norton & Company, 1994.

Mikaelian, Allen. *Medal of Honor: Profiles of America's Military Heroes from the Civil War to the Present.* New York: Hyperion, 2002.

Murty, Marlene Reckling. *Mary Edwards Walker, M.D.* Arlington: The Women in Military Service for America Memorial Foundation, Inc., 1994.

Snyder, Charles McCool. *Dr. Mary Walker: The Little Lady in Pants.* New York: Arno Press, 1974.

Stacey, Michelle. *The Fasting Girl.* New York: Jeremy P. Tarcher/Putnam, 2002.

The Sybil 4, no. 24 (15 June 1860).

Walker, Mary E. *Hit.* Amherst: Humanity Books, 2003 and 1871.

———. *Papers.* Syracuse University Special Collections, New York.

Walling, William H., A.M., M. D. *Sexology.* Philadelphia: Puritan Publishing Company, 1904.

Wright, Fred P. "Dr. Mary E. Walker." Paper presented to the Oswego County Historical Society, NY, May 19, 1953.

Web sites

http://www.oswego.edu/library/archives/walker.pdf
A bibliography on Mary Edwards Walker, with a brief biography.

http://www.northnet.org/stlawrenceaauw/walker.htm
Brief biography of Walker with details of service to Union army, including Medal of Honor.

http://www.army.mil/cmh/mohciv2.htm
The U.S. Army Web site features a full citation to Walker's Medal of Honor award (in context of Civil War medal winners M-Z).

http://sunsite.utk.edu/civil-war/warweb.html
A comprehensive collection of Web sites relating to all aspects of the American Civil War.

Index